13 Things
You
Gotta
Know

To Make It As A Christian

13 Things You Gotta Know

To Make It As A Christian

Josh McDowell & Bob Hostetler

WORD PUBLISHING
Dallas · London · Vancouver · Melbourne

Thirteen Things You Gotta Know

Library of Congress Cataloging-in-Publication Data

McDowell, Josh.
    Thirteen things you gotta know : a PowerLink student devotional featuring the characters from the novel *Under Siege* / Josh McDowell and Bob Hostetler.
    p. cm.
    Summary: A collection of devotional readings spanning thirteen weeks, providing insight into the characters of the novel *Under Siege* and promoting daily prayer and Bible reading.
    ISBN 0–8499–3413–3
    1. Teenagers—Prayer-books and devotions—English.
2. Devotional calendars. [1. Prayer books and devotions.
2. Christian life.] I. Hostetler, Bob, 1958– . II. McDowell, Josh. *Under Siege*. III. Title.
BV4850.M2836 1992
242'.63—dc20   92–33490
                                                     CIP
                                                     AC

3 4 5 9 LB 9 8 7 6 5 4 3
Printed in the United of America

Contents

How to Use This Book

The selections in this book offer an exciting companion to *The PowerLink Chronicles: Under Siege.*

Each chapter will give dramatic insight into a different character from *Under Siege,* and will follow the dramatic portion of the devotional with a "PowerLink/PowerThink" segment offering a chance to apply that chapter's emphasis to your life in thought, word, and deed. If you haven't already read *Under Siege,* we urge you to do so. However, it is not necessary to read *Under Siege* before reading this Devotional.

We suggest that you read one chapter at the beginning of each week and fully apply yourself to the "PowerLink/ PowerThink" portion on that day. For the next six days, we have provided a very brief suggestion to help you develop a daily habit of prayer and Bible reading. Using this book for the next thirteen weeks will help establish you in the faith and continue the work God has begun in you.

God is the one who saves me; I will trust him and not be afraid.

Isaiah 12:2

1

Marlon's Dilemma

Marlon's eyes flipped open like the headlights of a sports car. He knew he was awake, although it felt like he was dreaming. The events of last night seemed so long ago and far away.

He had run into Will McConnell, his computer science class partner, at the mall. Will had surprised Marlon with an invitation to get a Coke together.

Marlon was surprised at the invitation. He was one of the geekiest-looking sophomores at Eisenhower High. He was short and chunky, his clothes always looked about three fads behind the times, and he didn't socialize well. But he was a computer whiz and had been helpful to Will. Five minutes later they were sitting at a small table in the middle of the noisy food park next to Santa's Workshop.

After some small talk, Will cleared his throat and looked Marlon in the eye. "Marlon, this being Christmas and all, do you ever think about spiritual things like God and heaven and stuff?"

Marlon's face darkened slightly at the question. "No, not really. My parents dragged me to Sunday school when I was little. That's when my real dad was alive. But now my stepdad watches sports on Sunday mornings. So I usually sleep in or work on the computer game I'm inventing."

"Yeah," Will said, "God didn't used to be very important to me either. I've gone to church most of my life, but it's been more of a ritual than a relationship with God. But something happened at the end of summer this year that changed all that—changed me, too. Can I tell you about it?"

Marlon looked more curious than skeptical, and he nodded.

Will briefly told about the youth group campout and some things that had happened after that. "So just before school started I opened my life to God's love and forgiveness like never before. Celebrating Christ's birthday this year is something special to me because I'm learning to make Him the center of my life."

Will paused. Marlon felt like a computer program that suddenly locked. He could think of nothing to do or say.

After a few moments of awkward silence, Will went on. "Speaking of Christ, Marlon, if you died today, do you know for sure that you would go to heaven?"

"What? Today?" Marlon said. "How should I know?"

"Would you like to know for sure?"

"Well . . . yeah," Marlon said with a nod of his head. "Who wouldn't?"

Will took a small, well-worn booklet out of his wallet. He read it to Marlon, explaining about God's love, the problem of sin, God's solution, and the importance of trusting Christ personally.

"Is there any reason why you wouldn't want to trust Christ as your own personal Lord and Savior right now, Marlon?" Will concluded.

Marlon looked away and shifted uncomfortably, saying nothing. His mind was racing, searching for some sort of excuse or escape.

Tell him you need to think about it, a voice said inside him. Then, just as quickly, another voice suggested, *Tell him you're supposed to meet somebody.*

Finally, he turned back abruptly to face Will. "No, there's no reason at all. I'm ready."

At a small table in the middle of the mall's food park, right there next to Santa's Workshop, Marlon quietly prayed to trust Christ and claim His salvation.

Now, less than twelve hours later, Marlon stared at the ceiling above his bed. *What happened last night?* he thought. *It was like something I just watched on television.*

He swung his legs onto the floor and sat up, resting his elbows on his knees. His gaze rested on his thick legs and arms. He turned his hands over several times in front of him.

Still the same old Marlon. Nothing's changed. I sure don't feel any different, anyway. Nope, it's just another Sunday morning.

"Sunday morning! Oh, man!" He looked at the clock. "Oh, man," he repeated. He jumped to his feet and ran into the bathroom.

Marlon was still getting dressed when Will's mother honked the horn. Will had been pretty adamant that Marlon get into a church fellowship once his decision to follow Christ had been made, and he'd told Marlon matter-of-factly that he and his mom would be picking him up to go to church with them—at least for a while.

As Marlon sat through the Sunday school class and morning worship, those nagging doubts continued to creep into his head. *Why don't I feel any different?* During worship, he looked around at the sanctuary full of people. *Maybe I'm not really a Christian like all these other people. Maybe it didn't "take" like it's supposed to. It did seem awfully simple last night—maybe I didn't do it right.*

By the time he arrived home Sunday after church, Marlon was thoroughly discouraged and nearly convinced that his prayer of salvation the night before hadn't "worked."

◆ ◆ ◆

Marlon talked with Will several times over the Christmas break, and shared some of the things he'd been thinking about. He liked being with Will. He really did feel like he was learning some things, but he still had trouble with those doubts.

"I know I should stop doubting and just believe," Marlon said, "but I can't get over this idea that I'm fooling myself, that it's not real."

"Did you look up those Bible verses I wrote down for you?"

"Yeah."

"*And?*"

"Well, I guess they helped all right, but I still feel like I should be able to *know* I'm saved, right?"

"Yeah," Will answered, a little irritation surfacing in his voice. "Marlon, you remember that train diagram I showed you, with FACT as the engine and FAITH as the middle car and FEELING as the caboose?" Marlon nodded. "You're still putting your feelings ahead of the facts. What are the facts?"

Marlon stared blankly at Will.

"Maybe I'm in over my head, Marlon. I don't know what else to say to you."

"No, it's not your fault, Will. I *know* that God and His Word are the facts and that I've confessed my sins. . . ."

"And He's forgiven you?"

"Yeah."

"And He's living in you?"

"Yeah. I know all that, and I believe it—I guess I do—but I'm just having a hard time with it, you know."

Marlon knew that Will was getting discouraged with him.

"Guess I better go check the mail," he said, knowing as he said it that Will knew he just didn't want to talk any more.

Marlon said goodbye to Will at the mailbox, then walked slowly back to the house, absently thumbing through the envelopes.

"Junk," he muttered.

He paused in front of the steps to read the promises on the outside of a sweepstakes envelope: "You've won a million dollars (if our computer selects one of your sweepstakes numbers below)! Buy that dream house, that boat, that car you've always wanted!"

Marlon stared at the colorful envelope. His brain seemed to click like a computer running a memory check, until finally his thought completed itself.

"What if I won a million dollars?" he speculated. "Would I *feel* rich? What would it be like?"

He sat down on the steps.

"Would I wonder if I were *really* rich? How would I know for sure?"

He pondered the question for a moment.

"I guess I would just *know*, right?"

He stood.

"No," he said. "No, I'd just check my bankbook. If I had any doubts about being rich, I'd just dig out my bankbook. It would tell me the truth."

His conversation with Will seemed a little silly to him now.

"I don't have to *feel* saved to know I'm saved. If I can trust a bank and bankbook, surely I can believe God and His Word. It's not about *feelings*, it's about *facts*."

He turned the sweepstakes envelope around in his hands. "Maybe I'll ask Mom if I can keep this—put it in my Bible."

He walked into the house to call Will.

PowerLink   PowerThink

Marlon's struggle is painfully common among new Christians. If you have recently come to trust in Christ, you've probably encountered the same doubts:

Am I really saved?

Has anything really changed?

Why don't I feel any different?

Maybe I'm not really a Christian.

Maybe it didn't 'take' like it's supposed to.

Maybe I didn't do it right.

Such doubts are common. The first thing Satan and his agents try to do after a person trusts in Christ for salvation is to create doubt that anything *real* happened.

But a Christian doesn't have to *feel* his salvation in order to *have* salvation. A Christian doesn't have to *feel* different in order to *be* different, any more than a millionaire has to feel rich in order to be rich.

Take a few minutes to absorb the assurance of your salvation in thought, word and deed:

- How does trusting God for salvation compare to trusting a bank to keep your wealth safe for you? In what ways are the two different?

- How does Marlon's analogy of the bankbook strike you? How might a bankbook be like the Bible? How is it different?

- Read 2 Timothy 1:12. Paul says "I know Jesus, the One I have believed in. . . ." Why does he say that and not, "I know *what* I have believed"? He also says, "I am sure that he is able to protect what he has trusted me with until that day." What does Paul's imagery have in common with Marlon's? What was God able to protect? What has God trusted *you* with? Are you convinced that He is able to protect it until the day of His coming?

- Read Isaiah 12:2. Why does the writer think it necessary to say, "*God* is the one who saves me?" Write that verse below.

Now read it aloud, slowly.

- When Satan attacks you and creates doubt about your salvation, look up Isaiah 12:2 and read it aloud several times. You may want to copy it onto a card to carry in your purse or wallet, or even memorize it.

- Pray this Scripture-based prayer aloud:

  Father, You are the One who saves me. Help me to trust and not be afraid. You give me strength and make me sing, You have saved me.[1] Help me draw near to You with a sincere heart and a sure faith.[2] Let your salvation take root in my heart, not only with words, but also with power, with the Holy Spirit and with sure knowledge that is true.[3] In the name of Jesus, I pray, Amen.

- Day 2   Read 2 Thessalonians 2:13–17 and close in prayer:

  Father, please comfort me and strengthen me in every good thing I do and say today. Please give me hope and comfort in the knowledge of my salvation. Amen.

- Day 3   Read 2 Timothy 1:9–12 and follow with prayer:

  Father, help me to trust You to protect what You've given to me until the day of Christ's return. Amen.

---

1. Isaiah 12:2
2. Hebrews 10:22
3. 1 Thessalonians 2:5

- Day 4   Read Hebrews 10:22–23. Close with a prayer of thanks for the blessings mentioned in those verses.

- Day 5   Read 1 Peter 1:3–9 and spend a few moments praising God for His blessings before presenting your requests to Him.

- Day 6   Read 1 John 3:19–24. Present your requests to God, then close with a prayer of thanksgiving based on those verses of Scripture.

- Day 7   Read 1 John 5:13–15, 18–20. After a few moments of personal prayer, close with:

Thank You, Father, for the assurance that I belong to You—today and forever. Amen.

But if we confess our sins, he will forgive our sins, because we can trust God to do what is right. He will cleanse us from all the wrongs we have done.

1 John 1:9

2

Amber's Dream

Amber's tall, slender figure emerged from her tent, wearing an oversized football jersey. She paused for just a moment and listened to the sounds of the night. Everyone else at the youth group campout seemed to be asleep. She peered through the shadows, then crept away toward the beach.

She reached the shoreline and followed it a little way, until she turned from the shoreline and began angling toward the trees. A light flickered in the darkness.

The dim light of a small flashlight aimed at a sawed-off tree stump. Amber joined the three silhouettes behind the light. Tony Ortiz, Reggie Spencer, and Krystal Wayne huddled together on a log around a stack of beer cans on the stump.

"I knew you wouldn't want to miss out on the fun," Tony said to Amber, handing her a can and pulling the tab. Amber took the can, but Tony, who appeared a little unsteady on his feet, wrapped his arms around her before she could take a sip.

"And the fun's just beginning. Right, Krystal?" Reggie said, slurring his words slightly. Krystal giggled a response, then the two of them fell together in a long kiss, punctuated with a deft move of Reggie's hands inside Krystal's shirt.

Tony kissed Amber lightly on the cheek, then on the mouth. Amber cooperated, but while Tony wrestled with her, she wrestled with a shaky feeling in the pit of her stomach. Tony drank from Amber's can and encouraged her to take a sip. She did, but quickly put her hand to her mouth as if gagging on the stuff.

Tony took the can from Amber's hand. "This is what you really need, Baby," he said as he folded her into his arms and kissed her forcefully on the mouth. Amber reached up and embraced him.

Her mind reeled like a carnival Tilt-O-Wheel. *Do I really want to do this?* she thought. *Yes!* came the answer at first. *Tony is so perfect, I'd be crazy not to let it happen.*

Tony leaned back with Amber in his arms until they lay on the ground, their legs curled over the log.

I should just let it happen, she told herself. *I'm a big girl now, and nobody's here to tell me what I can't do.* Tony interrupted her thoughts with a nibble on her neck. Amber lowered her shoulders, which had been lifted slightly off the ground, and felt herself relax. Tony noticed her response and began to move to capitalize on the opportunity.

Amber felt a sinking sensation, as though she were disappearing into the ground beneath her. A voice in her head told her she'd let Tony go too far to turn back now; she might as well surrender to the moment.

A twig cracked in the distance.

Amber snapped her head off the ground.

"It's nothing, Baby," Tony said, without interrupting his attentions to Amber.

Once it's done, it's done, Amber thought. *Will I be sorry if I do this? Will I be sorry if I don't?*

She raised herself on her elbows. Tony applied pressure to her neck with a kiss to coax her back to her former position.

"Tony," she whispered.

He ignored her.

"Tony," she repeated.

"Baby—"

"Let me up, Tony."

"I told you it's nothing, Baby. Don't worry about it. Don't spoil the mood."

She slid her hand between them and pushed him away.

"I'm going back to the tent." She stood. He reached for her hand.

"I'm sorry, Tony," she said as she drew her hand away from him. "I'm going back."

Amber stumbled through the trees and followed the beach along her former path. She glanced around before entering her tent. Everything appeared peaceful.

Darcelle was awake. Amber felt her open eyes the moment she entered the dark tent. She sat down on her sleeping bag and felt her insides quiver nervously and guiltily.

"Anything you wanna talk about?" Darcelle asked.

"No," Amber whispered, then quickly corrected herself. "Yes."

With a trembling voice, Amber told Darcelle everything that had happened that night. Darcelle only spoke a few quiet words when she had finished, and they both sat in silence for a while.

Amber broke the silence.

"I feel like God can never forgive me."

Darcelle opened her mouth to speak, but Amber spoke again.

"I *know* I can never forgive myself."

Darcelle faced Amber squarely and told her God *could* forgive her, and *would* if she would just confess her sin to Him and seek His forgiveness.

"You don't understand, Darcelle. You've never done the things I've done."

"I've done worse, Amber—a lot worse, if any sin can be worse than another." Darcelle shared with Amber some of the events that led her to an abortion and a miscarriage in her eighth-grade year. Amber listened, but couldn't seem to translate Darcelle's experiences into terms that could make her believe she could be forgiven.

"It's not just tonight, Darcelle; I've been doing a lot of things—worse and worse things."

They talked and prayed for hours. It was after one o'clock in the morning when Liz peeked into their tent. She explained that she'd heard their voices and wanted to make sure everything was all right. When they filled Liz in on what had been going on and what they'd been talking about, she said, "The Lord must've known to keep me awake tonight."

She went on to explain a little bit about her background and how, even after she had become a Spirit-filled Christian in college, she still struggled to grasp God's forgiveness and forgive herself, too.

"But whether or not *you* know it—as a matter of fact, no matter *how* you feel or think—when you repent, God forgives you. It's as simple as that. Now, your hesitance to forgive yourself may make it hard to really believe that, but it's true even if you don't believe it.

"I think it's sort of like a fancy hotel I was in once. My room had an inside door. When I opened it, there was another door. My door locked on my side and that door locked on the other side; they did it that way so that the rooms could be shared, like among families, but both doors had to be open in order for there to be a doorway through.

"Repentance," Liz continued, "opens God's door. When you confess your sins and repent of them, God opens that door wide. Even if you can't forgive yourself, God's door is still open—He still forgives you. And when you *do* forgive yourself and open your door, you'll find His is already open—like it always was."

Amber raised a tear-stained face to Liz. Her shoulders shook slightly with emotion as Liz and Darcelle each put an arm around her. The trio sat in the tent and prayed.

After Liz had left and Darcelle slid into her sleeping bag, Amber lay on her back thinking, crying, and staring at the canvas over her head for a few moments.

As she closed her eyes, he saw the doors that Liz had described. She stood on one side, before a door covered on all sides with padlocks, deadbolts, and key locks. In her dream she began to unlock them, and with each one she heard her own voice reciting the sins of her past, sins for which she had never forgiven herself. As she unlocked her way around the door frame and back to where she thought she had begun, new locks seemed to appear. She feared she'd never finish, that there were too many locks, that they would never stop materializing.

She began to sweat. The keys and bolts grew more difficult to work. She began to breathe heavily, and her fingers started to hurt. She continued, however, working faster, every moment more determined. She recited her sins through gritted teeth until—she paused for a moment, not believing what she was seeing—she gripped the last lock on the door. She slid her hand along the doorframe, as if waiting for more locks to appear. She then squeezed the bolt tightly in her right hand, and grunted out, "I forgive you for the drinking and groping in the woods with Tony."

Amber snapped to a sitting position on her sleeping bag. She exhaled as if a bucket of ice water had been thrown on her.

"Darcelle!" She grabbed the sleeping form next to her and shook her friend. Darcelle rolled over on one elbow.

"What time is it, Darcelle? I want to remember this exactly—I know I'm forgiven, Darcelle! He forgives me! Oh God, thank You. He forgives me!"

===

PowerLink   PowerThink

Some Christians have no problem understanding and believing God's forgiveness of their sins. Many others, however, find it very difficult to really believe that, when they've confessed their sins and repented, God freely forgives.

You can fully experience God's forgiveness, no matter what you think of yourself. Start by making sure of a few simple steps:

1. Remember that God loves you unconditionally. You are His special child. He paid a high price—the death of His one and only Son, Jesus Christ—to reclaim you as His child. Your forgiveness was expensive, but God paid the price willingly (Romans 5:8).

As a Christian, when you are disobedient, you grieve God (Ephesians 4:29–32). But His love for you never changes. He may discipline you to draw you near to Him (Hebrews 12:5–12), but His love stays consistent and perfect.

The problem is your sin, which is expressed in your attitudes and actions. The logical question, then, is, "How can I experience God's love and forgiveness when I sin?"

2. Confess your sin. Even though you are a Christian, you can still be hassled by what the Bible calls your "sin nature" (Romans 7:20–25). And as you allow your sin nature to have dominance in your life instead of God, the result is disobedience on your part—and a lot of unhappiness.

But God has provided a solution for your occasional lack of faith and disobedience . According to God's Word, the solution begins with confession (1 John 1:9). To confess means to agree with God that your disobedience and lack of faith is sin. God is well aware of your attitudes and actions. But He is waiting for you to agree with Him. By doing so, you humble yourself before God and experience God's grace and power (1 Peter 5:5–6).

3. Claim God's forgiveness. Confession does not mean you receive more of God's forgiveness. Christ has already forgiven you once and for all through His death on the cross (Hebrews 10:12–14; 1 Peter 3:18). You can't get more forgiveness. Rather, you must claim and accept the forgiveness that is already yours.

In claiming God's forgiveness you accept by faith what God has said to you in His Word. As you do, He will help you experience the incredible truth of your forgiveness in your life. It's like discovering a treasure that was always yours because it was buried in your own backyard. You are loved and forgiven by God. Claim it and enjoy it!

- What do you think is harder: to believe God has forgiven you or to forgive yourself? Why?

- Do you think God's forgiveness helps you forgive yourself or does forgiving yourself help you experience God's forgiveness?

- Read John 8:1–11. What had the woman's sin been? How did Jesus respond to her sin? Why didn't He condemn her? Why did He tell her to stop sinning?

- Read 1 John 1:9. What condition of forgiveness does this verse mention (hint: look for the word "if")? Once you confess, what does your forgiveness depend on? What causes it to happen? What else does this verse promise that God will do for you?

The following verses each have three words in common. Read each one and *after each verse* write those three words:

2 Chronicles 7:14 _I will forgive_

Jeremiah 31:34 _I will forgive_

Hebrews 8:12 _I will forgive_

- Write 1 John 1:9 on an index card or slip of paper that you can carry in your purse or pocket. Read it several times a day until you've committed it to memory.

- Pause for a few moments of prayer, and ask the Holy Spirit to reveal to you any sins from your past for which you need to seek forgiveness. Imagine each one as a lock on a door, and pray patiently through each one that God brings to mind until you can swing the door of God's forgiveness open and claim the assurance of His complete and unconditional love.

- Day 2   Read Acts 13:38–39 and follow with prayer:

  Father, I praise You because You're a forgiving God. Thank You for forgiving me. Please make me more aware of Your forgiveness. Amen.

- Day 3   Read Ephesians 1:3–7. Next, *pray* those verses, inserting the pronoun "me" in place of "us."

- Day 4   Read Colossians 1:9–14. Turn Paul's prayer into *yours,* praying (for example) "Lord, help my love to grow more and more . . . " and so on.

- Day 5   Read Colossians 3:12–13 and spend a few moments praising God for His blessings before presenting your requests to Him.

- Day 6   Read 1 John 1:5–9. Close by praying:

  Father, You are light and in You is no darkness at all. Help me to live in the light of Your love and forgiveness. Amen.

- Day 7   Read Jude 24–25. After a few moments of personal prayer, close with:

    Thank You, Father, that You are strong and can help me not to fall, that You can bring me before Your glory without any wrong in me, and give me great joy. You are the only God. You are the One who saves me. I give You glory, greatness, power, and authority through Jesus Christ my Lord for all time past, now, and forever. Amen.

But you are not ruled by your sinful selves. You are ruled by the Spirit, if that Spirit of God really lives in You.

Romans 8:9

3

Liz's Discovery

Liz slapped her dance partner, a twenty-year-old philosophy major named Shawn. He laid his hand on the side of his face, where the skin was turning red with pain and embarrassment.

"What's wrong with you?" he said, stepping away from her.

"I told you I don't do that stuff anymore," she whispered.

A few heads in the crowded bar turned their direction, but the music drowned their conversation; they could almost shout in complete privacy.

"Liz Perry, you little hypocrite," he said. "You come with your usual squeeze to your usual bar and have your usual drink, and still try to tell me you're different now, that you don't put out anymore."

She slapped him again, on the same cheek. He lunged for her. Liz thought he would hit her with his balled fist, but instead he grabbed her roughly by a wrist and began dragging her across the dance floor toward the door.

"No! Let go of me, you—you—" She screamed and fought, trying to scratch Shawn's arms and face with her fingernails. He yanked her arm with such force she was afraid he'd break it. The journey to the door seemed to take forever, and Liz wondered *Doesn't anybody see what's happening? Isn't anybody going to help me?*

Just before they reached the exit, a muscular man appeared and said something Liz couldn't hear. The trio froze for a moment, as Shawn and the man glared at each other, and Liz held her breath and stared at them both. Finally, Shawn threw

Liz's wrist back at her and stomped out the door.

Later that night, Liz sat crying in her friend Sarah's dorm room.

"I can't do it, Sarah," she said between sobs, "I guess I just can't do it."

"You *can* do it, Liz. It's just—what made you go to Casey's in the first place?"

"I don't know. I get to where sometimes I—I need an outlet or something. I've tried, but I can't seem to be good like you, Sarah. Maybe I've been drinking and partying too long. Maybe it's too late to quit."

"Liz, remember what Duane's been discussing in our study and prayer group? Being a Christian isn't just about do's and don'ts. It's not about 'being good.' It's about a relationship. And the deeper and stronger you get in that relationship, the easier it'll be to live a Christian life."

Liz nodded her head, but the expression on her face told Sarah that she wasn't too hopeful.

Liz had trusted Christ as a result of Sarah's invitation to a prayer group led by Duane Cunningham, an enthusiastic student who always seemed to be smiling at her. After a few evenings with the group, she gave in to the acceptance and love she felt from them and prayed to receive salvation. She left the prayer group that night with her head throbbing from the tears she'd shed and her heart pounding with excitement and joy. The first week or two of her experience made her feel like she'd never really lived before, like she was suddenly waking from a coma.

But now she felt that her new life as a Christian was crumbling. Every morning when she woke up, she determined to live a Christian life—a life just like her friend Sarah's. But her good intentions always seemed to waver, and by the weekend she would often be drinking and partying as she had always done.

Now, as she walked back to her dorm after talking and praying with Sarah, she was convinced she could never change her behavior.

"I'm just a failure as a Christian, " she told herself. "Some people can do it, maybe, but not me. I guess I'm just not strong enough or something."

Her thoughts were interrupted by the revving engine of a sporty red convertible that pulled to the curb beside her and slowed to her walking pace.

"Liz! C'mon, we're heading over to Beefcakes. It's ladies' night."

Liz opened her mouth to speak, but only let out a sigh. She looked absently up and down the sidewalk.

"Get in!" the driver roared.

Without a word, she climbed into the car.

She knew she was going off the deep end now, but Liz felt she had nothing left to fight with. She drank without thinking, and danced and talked with a forced gaiety. When her friends decided to leave, Liz waved them away.

"I'm not ready yet," she said with a shrill, slurred voice.

She sat, unmoving, until the bartender approached her and asked if she had a ride or if there was anyone he could call for her.

Sarah's face wore an expression Liz had never seen when she arrived to take Liz home.

"Let's go," she snapped. Sarah wheeled around and marched out the door.

Sarah strode to her car, opened the passenger door, and stood impatiently as Liz stumbled across the parking lot. When Liz finally reached the car, Sarah stood in front of the open door.

"So this is how a Christian acts, huh?" she said, placing her nose just inches away from Liz's face.

"I don't know, why don't you tell me," Liz retorted sarcastically, trying to push Sarah aside.

"How can you do this, Liz? How can you—"

"Shut up! Shut up!" she shouted several times, punctuating her screams with obscenities until she began sobbing between words and her shouts died into a tearful whimper.

Sarah pulled Liz into her arms and held her close.

"What makes you do this, Liz? How can you say such things?"

Liz cried harder, and Sarah squeezed her tighter.

"How can you talk that way to me?" Sarah asked, hurt rising in her voice.

Liz sniffed loudly, raised her head, and wiped her eyes with her wrist.

"I . . . I'm sorry, Sarah. I only talk like that when I've had too much to drink. It's like it's not even me talking, you know? It's the alcohol. . . it changes me."

Sarah snapped to attention.

"What?" Liz asked, looking around her to see what had caused Sarah to stiffen.

"Say what you just said."

"What?"

"What you said about it's like it's not you talking."

"Yeah. . . ." Liz stretched the word out while she thought. "It's like it's not even me. It's the drink."

"Right," Sarah said, her eyes brightening. "Ephesians something-or-other."

"What?"

"I don't know where it is, but it's in Ephesians somewhere, in the New Testament. 'Be not drunk with wine, wherein is excess, but be filled with the Spirit. . . .'"

Liz was calmer now.

"I have no idea what you're talking about, Sarah."

"Well, you said that when you have too much to drink, you act differently, in a way that isn't like you at all."

"Uh huh."

"All you have to do is fill yourself with alcohol and certain things come out in your actions and your talk that otherwise don't come naturally to you at all, right?"

Liz nodded, but her face still wore a puzzled expression.

"Maybe that's what that verse from Ephesians means. I never thought about it that way before, but the same way that filling yourself with booze makes you behave differently, if you were to fill yourself with the Holy Spirit, *He* would make certain things come out in your life that otherwise don't come naturally at all. You've been *wanting* to live a Christian life, right?"

"Well . . .yeah."

"Don't you get it? All you have to do to make a Christian

life happen in you is to fill yourself with the Spirit. Let Him control you every day!"

"And then," Liz interrupted, measuring her words carefully, "and then He'd make me act Christian the same way alcohol makes me act—well, like I just did?"

"Well, yeah, pretty much. See, the point is, you don't have to *try* to live a Christian life . . . the Spirit will live it in you, if you're filled with Him."

"Okay, but how? How do I do that?"

Sarah stepped aside to let Liz into the car.

"Get in," she said. "Let's go back to my room."

PowerLink   PowerThink

Living the Christian life isn't hard, it's impossible. In fact, there's only one Person who has ever lived a perfect Christian life, and that was Jesus Christ Himself.

Maybe that's why we're called Christians. The word Christian actually means "Christ in you." The only way you can live the Christian life is by allowing Christ to take up residence inside you and develop His qualities through you. That's supernatural, but then again, that's what Christianity and being a disciple is all about.

Like Liz, all new Christians have a lot to learn about letting Christ live within us. The Bible actually calls it the Spirit-filled life. Let's take a look at this Person who is so vital to our walk with God—the Holy Spirit.

- The Bible teaches us that the Holy Spirit is God's Spirit. If that is true, does that mean that the Holy Spirit is a thing? a force? a presence? a person?

- It is through the Holy Spirit that God does His work in our lives. For example, the Holy Spirit enables us to understand the Bible (John 14:26). He gives us courage and the words we need to share Christ with others (Acts 1:8). And He develops in us the qualities that make us winners in our relationship with God and with others. In light of all that, what might happen if a new Christian has an incomplete or mistaken understanding of the Holy Spirit?

- Read Romans 8:9. What does this verse say is true of "you"? What is the condition (hint: look for the word "if")? The "Spirit" is referred to three times in this verse, but in three different ways. Write them below:

What significance does that have to you?

- Read Ephesians 5:18. Why do you think Paul mentioned being drunk with wine and being filled with the Spirit in the same verse?

- Read 2 Corinthians 1:21–22. Paul uses an analogy in these verses much like the analogy Marlon used in chapter one. To what does he compare the Spirit and His role in our lives?

• You must allow the Holy Spirit to fill you and take charge of your life. How do you do that? Here are three simple principles that will help you be filled by and walk in the power of God's Holy Spirit.

1. Confess your sin (1 John 1:9). The Holy Spirit cannot fill and lead you when you choose to live your life independent from God. That's why many Christians face such frustration.

Whenever you realize that you have been disobedient to God and are in control of your life, you must agree that your independence is wrong. By faith, claim God's love and the forgiveness for sin He has promised you.

2. Trust God to fill you and lead you by His Spirit. For a lot of Christians, knowing God's love and forgiveness and acting on them every day can be two different things. God calls us to respond to His love by allowing Him to be Lord of our lives and letting Him fill us with His Spirit. Being filled with the Spirit means that He is directing our lives and giving us His power to resist temptation, gain courage, make right choices, and deal with everything that happens in our lives each day. The word "filled" means to be permeated or controlled by the Holy Spirit who lives within you.

What must you do to be filled with (controlled by) the Holy Spirit?

First, you must present every area of your life to God (Romans 12:1–2). Ask God to help you identify every area of your life—activities, friends, desires, and so forth—and ask Him to be your leader in each area.

Second, ask the Holy Spirit to fill you. God commands us to be filled with the Holy Spirit (Ephesians 5:18). Asking to be filled is a clear step of obedience.

Third, believe that He fills you when you ask Him to. The Holy Spirit is a free gift to be received. As you pray and express your request to be filled, God promises to answer (1 John 5:14–15).

Is it God's will for you to be filled with His Spirit? Yes. Will He fill you if you ask Him to? You can count on it! Will you feel differently when you are filled with God's Spirit? Not necessarily. Being filled with the Spirit is not so much a matter of *feeling* as it is a matter of *fact*. God fills us because He promises to do so in His Word. That's fact! Feelings come and go. The greatest evidence of God's control in your life is the peace, power, and fruit of the Spirit you will experience.

3. Keep walking in the Spirit. Just because you trust God to fill you with His Spirit doesn't mean that you will never blow it through lack of faith or disobedience. No one is perfect. And besides, you have that old sinful nature, a sinful world around you, and even the devil himself to contend with. But you can live more consistently day after day if you apply these simple principles.

First, when you blow it, confess your sin quickly and turn back to God. Ask Him to fill you again with His Spirit and trust Him to do so. Keep short accounts with God. The longer you put off dealing with sin in your life, the more distant you become in your walk with God. And when you sense a distance between you and God, who moved? You did! Move back right away.

Second, build your faith through your study of God's Word and through prayer (Romans 10:17). Your involvement in these disciplines is vital to your faith. They cleanse and transform your mind and disarm Satan's tactics. Set aside a regular time every day to involve yourself in Bible study and prayer.

Third, be prepared for spiritual conflict against the world (1 John 2:15–17), the flesh (Galatians 5:16–21), and Satan (1 Peter 5:8–9). Instead of gritting your teeth and *trying*, respond to the conflict by relying on God's Spirit working in you and through you—*relying* instead of *trying*.

Take a few moments right now to pray a simple prayer for the filling of the Holy Spirit:

Dear Father, I need You. I acknowledge that I have been directing my life and that, as a result, I have sinned against You. I thank You that You have forgiven my sins through Christ's death on the cross for me. I now invite Christ to again take His place on the throne of my life. Fill me with the Holy Spirit as You commanded me to be filled, and as You promised in Your Word that You would do if I asked in faith. I now thank You for directing my life and for filling me with the Holy Spirit.

- Day 2   Read Luke 11:5–13. Follow with a prayer thanking God for the gift of His Holy Spirit.

- Day 3   Read Acts 1:1–8. Spend a few moments contemplating those verses before praying for your needs and the needs of those around you.

- Day 4   Read Romans 7:14–25. Follow with prayer, telling God frankly about your frustrations and discouragements.

- Day 5   Read Romans 8:1–11. Then pray:

    Father, thank You for giving me life through Your Spirit, who lives in me. I submit to Him and His control.

Now present your requests to God and close with prayers of praise.

- Day 6   Read Romans 8:12–17. Close with a prayer committing today to God.

- Day 7   Read Romans 8:22–31. After a few moments of personal prayer, close with:

    Thank You, Father, for the assurance that if You are with me, no one can defeat me. Please continue to teach me how to use the Spirit's help to stop doing wrong. Help me to let Him lead. Amen.

The only temptation that has come to you is that which everyone has. But you can trust God, who will not permit you to be tempted more than you can stand. But when you are tempted, he will also give you a way to escape so that you will be able to stand it.

1 Corinthians 10:13

4

Will's Struggle

The fantasies had begun again.

Ever since Will McConnell's relationship with Amber Lockwood had begun to warm, the temptation to fantasize about her had flared, too. Not that this was some blazing love affair. After all, they had only held hands three or four times, hugged only once—more from joy than from passion—and never even come close to a kiss. But Will was certain that Amber's interest in him had grown beyond the brother-sister stage of a month ago.

That excited him, of course, but he was starting to worry about the direction his thoughts were taking lately.

He'd always loved to imagine things about him and Amber. *Who wouldn't?* he rationalized. She was tall and slender, with shoulder-length black hair, full eyebrows that arched enchantingly over her mysterious green eyes, and a well-tanned figure.

But Will had recently given Christ control of his life, and had even committed his relationship with Amber to Him.

So why am I still having these thoughts? he asked himself. Sometimes his daydreams just pictured Amber clutching his arm as they walked into Baskin-Robbins, laughing and gazing at him dreamily; at other times, he would imagine the two of them wrapped in a sweet embrace on a park bench under a starry sky. Lately, however, he would let his imagination carry him beyond romantic images to visions of lust and immorality.

39

Will had never told anyone about his fantasies, except his best friend. Jason knew his feelings about Amber, of course, and Will had never told him *all* the thoughts he'd had about her, but he had asked Jason for prayer and would occasionally tell Jason about his latest battle, an arrangement they'd made some time before—for several reasons.

But it seemed that every battle ended in defeat, and Will knew that he was letting the fantasies get too far. He began to put off going to bed, because that seemed to be the worst time for him. He would lie there tossing and turning, trying to focus on anything but the one thing his mind would always turn to. But even when he stayed awake to watch a late movie on television, reasoning that if he were tired enough he would fall asleep right away and not be alert enough to let his mind wander to those fantasies, a commercial or a scene in the movie would inevitably ignite the very thoughts he wished to avoid.

The temptation would strike him in Amber's presence, too. Will knew she never encouraged it, but he would often flush in her presence, fearing that she could somehow detect his thoughts.

"God," he would pray, "I know I'm not supposed to think these things. Please stop them from happening to me. I don't want to sin, but I just can't stop these thoughts from entering my head."

He found his attitude changing as the fantasies became more frequent and more dangerous.

"Maybe I'm making too big a deal out of it," he would tell himself. "After all, I'm not really *doing* anything. I've got plenty of temptation, but what have I actually *done*? I may be thinking about sin, but I'm not sinning."

For several days, Will justified himself with those words, telling himself that enjoying temptation was not the same thing as committing sin. At the same time, he began to neglect his time of devotions, knowing—but not quite admitting to himself—that prayer and Bible reading would be incompatible with those other things that had begun to occupy his mind.

During all his increasing problems with temptation, Will continued his involvement with the Liberation Commandos, and even managed to share the gospel with Tony Ortiz after a pizza party the group had planned.

At the Liberation Commandos meeting the following Monday, Will led the group in a prayer of thanksgiving for the victories they'd seen. He also shared—with genuine disappointment—how Tony had shown up after midnight and listened to a simple step-by-step gospel presentation but had run out suddenly without making a decision.

◆ ◆ ◆

Will rolled over in bed with a sleepy moan. The speakers on the shelf above his bed softly called to him. *Let me hold you, let me touch you, let me kiss you all through the night.* In his semi-consciousness state, Will realized that his Wounded Twinkie CD had been playing continuously as he slept. He hadn't listened to the Twinkie in months. But for some reason he slid the disc into his player late last night while doing homework, and then fell asleep without turning it off.

He knew it was time to get up for his morning devotions. But he snuggled under the covers to enjoy the warmth of his bed just a few minutes longer.

Somewhere in the twilight zone between sleeping and waking, Will saw himself seated on the platform in the school auditorium before the entire student body. He knew he was there to make a gospel presentation to the audience. But he found himself enjoying the speeches of those introducing him. Marlon Trask stepped to the podium and praised Will lavishly for leading him to Christ. Jason stood up and roasted him with a few good-natured jokes. Duane Cunningham was next, saying that Will was the most mature Christian boy he'd ever met.

Just as Will stepped to the podium to speak, the bell rang and the crowd quickly filed out of the auditorium. He was a little disappointed that he couldn't give his presentation. But he felt pretty good about the nice things everybody had said about him.

The auditorium finally emptied except for Will at the podium and a beautiful rally girl sitting in the front row smiling up at him. Amber was dressed in a white pullover sweater with a block red E on the front and a short, red pleated skirt.

Somewhere a band began playing a Wounded Twinkie song. Amber stood up and started singing the words to Will: "Let me hold you, let me touch you, let me kiss you all through the night." As she sang she danced a sexy dance that made Will boil with desire. With her eyes fixed on Will and her arms outstretched, she began moving slowly up the platform stairs.

"No, no, no!" Will yelped as he flew out of bed, suddenly fully awake. He lunged, and realized too late that his feet were crossed at the ankles, tangled in the sheet. He twisted in the air, reached for his feet, then fell in a jackknife dive. His nose met the rug before the rest of his body.

He lay on his side for a moment, wanting to curse and cry at the same time. Finally, he untangled his feet and scooted to the CD player.

He switched off the Twinkie, popped the CD out of the player, and flung it angrily across the room into his bookcase. "This is just what we were talking about last night," he muttered dejectedly. "Kick back for just a minute and the devil's there to pin you to the floor."

He rubbed his eyes and squinted at the clock. He should be heading out the door for school right now. He'd slept through devotions and breakfast. Will started for his closet, then turned and dropped to his knees beside his bed. "Lord, I admit that I've taken my eyes off You and focused on myself the last couple of days. And I know the devil would like to plant new seeds of pride and lust in me and spoil the good things You have done. But right now I resist Him in Your name and claim Your forgiveness. Help me encourage Marlon today and be a godly witness to Tony. Lord Jesus, continue to use me in Your rescue operation."

Will was dressed and out the door in five minutes. He wished he'd had more for breakfast than a toothbrush full of Crest.

PowerLink   PowerThink

The only Christians who don't face temptation are those who are already in heaven.

The rest of us must face temptation of one kind or another every single day of our lives. For new Christians, it can be particularly overwhelming. As Duane told the Liberation Commandos at their meeting the day after Easter, "The devil doesn't give up even though he's been defeated." The fact that you have experienced salvation through the Lord Jesus Christ will not cause Satan to sit on his hands and decide the game's all up with you. In fact, in many ways, a person's problems with temptation never really begin until he or she starts to respond to God's Holy Spirit.

"What do I do, then? How do I handle temptation? How can I avoid defeat when the devil tempts me?"

- What is the difference between temptation and sin? When does temptation become sin?

- Is it possible to "enjoy" a temptation without committing sin? Why or why not?

- Read Matthew 4:1–11. How did Jesus confront temptation? What was His defense? How long did He entertain the temptation before resisting? Do you think the devil tempted Jesus at His strongest or weakest points?

  Fill in the blanks below from 1 Corinthians 10:13:

  The only temptations that you have are *everyone*

  has

  But you can *trust God* .

  He will not let you be tempted *more than I can stand*

  But when you are tempted, God will also give you

  a way to escape .

  Then you will be able to *stand it* .

- Read Hebrews 2:17–18. According to verse 18, why is Jesus able to help those who are tempted?

- When you face temptation, do the following things in order to emerge victorious over temptation and sin:

1. *Be on your guard.* Expect temptation. Benjamin Franklin was wrong when he said, "in this world nothing is certain but death and taxes"—you can be certain that you'll be tempted, *especially* if you've recently trusted in Christ. "So be careful. Do not let those evil people lead you away by the wrong they do. Be careful so that you will not fall from your strong faith" (2 Peter 3:17).

2. *Respond to temptation quickly.* Part of Will's problem was that he *entertained* temptation. It's like entertaining a hungry lion; you may live a little while, but it'll soon turn on you and tear you to pieces. Notice that the account of Jesus' temptations seems to indicate that He responded to each temptation quickly—even immediately! Therein is a key to victory. "Do not give the devil a way to defeat you" (Ephesians 4:17).

3. *Submit to God.* When Will wised up, he went to his knees and submitted to God. It's not enough to turn from the temptation; you must also turn to God. Tell Him about your temptation and ask Him for His help (the very help He promises—see Hebrews 2:18).

4. *Resist the devil.* Once you have recognized the temptation and asked God's help in overcoming it, put your running shoes on and get out of there! Actively resist and rebuke the devil, and claim victory in the name of Jesus Christ. "So give yourselves to God," James wrote. "Stand against the devil, and the devil will run away from you" (James 4:7).

    And once He has helped you overcome, don't forget to thank God and praise Him for keeping His promise, because "you can trust God. He will not let you be tempted more than you can stand. But when you are tempted, God will also give you a way to escape that temptation" (1 Corinthians 10:13).

- Day 2   Read Matthew 26:36–41. Do you find verse 41 to be true in your life? Close with a prayer for strength against temptation.

- Day 3   Read Romans 6:8–14. Spend a few moments in prayer, offering yourself to God to be used for doing good. Afterward pray for your needs and the needs of those around you.

- Day 4   Read Ephesians 4:27. Follow with prayer:

  Father, thank You for Your presence and the strength You give me to resist temptation. Help me not to give the devil a way to defeat me, but turn my mind to prayer at the first sign of temptation. Amen.

- Day 5   Read Ephesians 6:10–13. Close with a prayer for the full armor of God.

- Day 6   Read James 1:12–18. After a few moments of personal requests, thank God for the lessons you've learned from defeat and the strength you've gained through victories over temptation this past week.

- Day 7   Read 2 Peter 2:4–9. Close with prayer:

  Father, You know how to save those who serve You. Save me today and every day from the tempter and his tricks. Amen.

He heals the brokenhearted and bandages their wounds.

Psalm 147:3

5

Joy's Past

Seven-year-old Joy cowered on her bed. Her quivering arms clasped a pillow in front of her, in which she buried her face.

The pillow muffled her childish moans and sobs, which sounded more like the cries of a wounded animal than anything human. She sat motionless in her bedroom for much of the afternoon, only occasionally lifting her head and wiping her eyes.

Shadows enveloped the room, as afternoon politely yielded to evening. Still Joy sat, sometimes silent and staring, at other times sobbing pitifully into her pillow.

Footsteps sounded in the hall outside her door. Joy lifted her head from the pillow to listen. The doorknob turned slowly, and Joy buried her face again. She heard, as if the sounds were broadcast over a gigantic loudspeaker, the door creak open and click closed, and the fall of heavy feet on her floor which stopped beside her bed.

She raised her head again, and she was crying. She peered up at her adopted father through frightened eyes.

"Please," she said, her trembling voice barely breaking the silence, "please not again."

◆ ◆ ◆

Seven years later . . . Liz placed a hand on Joy's back and began to rub circles just below her neck.

"Joy, I'm so sorry," she said. "I know those are hard memories to talk about."

Darcelle sat wordlessly on Joy's right side in Liz and Duane's apartment. The three had remained behind after a meeting of the youth group they called "The Liberation Commandos," and Duane had quickly disappeared to let them talk.

Joy's form convulsed with sobs, while Darcelle and Liz sat and cried with her.

"It still hurts so much," she finally told them. "Why does it still hurt so much?"

Darcelle and Liz exchanged glances. Liz pursed her lips and nodded her head. The crying continued, starting, dwindling, starting again.

Joy lifted her head and focused her reddened eyes on the wall opposite where she sat. She didn't look at either of her friends.

"I mean, if God's forgiven me—if Jesus died for me and all that—why does it still hurt? Why do I still have to hurt?"

"Joy." Liz spoke with a powerful softness in her voice that turned Joy's head. She looked directly into Liz's eyes, something she rarely did. "God forgives you for things *you* have done, for sins *you* have committed. It still hurts because you don't need forgiveness; you need healing."

Joy sniffed. "Healing?"

"Yes. Maybe not the kind you see on cable T.V., but—" She paused. "See, when you repented, God forgave you, right?"

Joy nodded slightly.

"He forgave you for all those sins in your past. But you still have hurts. And hurts hang on pretty stubbornly."

A sob erupted in Joy's throat, but she swallowed it and nodded her head again. "How do I get rid of the hurt?" she asked.

Liz sat silently for a few moments. Joy and Darcelle waited attentively.

"I think you start," Liz said, "by confronting your past."

"What do you mean?"

"Well, the first step you made toward forgiveness was by confronting your sin, right? Admitting it was there and then going to God with it."

Joy sat motionless. "I can't forgive them," she said. "I hate them, Liz. I wish I didn't, but I can't help it. I hate them."

Liz placed her hand on Joy's back again. "I think that's part of the reason why the hurt is still there, Joy. It's trapped deep down in you, and you won't get it out until you stop running from it and—"

"I can't, Liz." A sharp edge entered Joy's voice. "I know I should, but I will *never* forgive them—especially *him*—for what they did."

Joy and Darcelle prayed with Liz before leaving that night, but they all knew that Joy's struggle wasn't over. Joy felt that her hurt was justified. Anyone who'd been beaten and molested as she had would feel the same way, wouldn't they? She refused to forgive the man and woman who had adopted her. And even though most of the abuse was in the past now, Joy carried the pain and resentment inside her every day of her present.

Repeated conversations with Liz had not seemed to bring her any closer to confronting her past and dealing with her hurt. She still lived with her adoptive parents, and managed the daily routines of family life with a numb struggle. She prayed constantly, it seemed, for God to heal her; but the everyday agony endured.

God, why won't You take the pain from me? she prayed. *Why won't You just take it out of me? Take my bad memories, take my nightmares away, please.*

She reasoned with Liz, "If Jesus could heal blind people and cripples and stuff like that, why can't He heal me? I mean, they didn't have to *do* anything, did they?"

She argued with Darcelle, "It wasn't my fault, Darcelle. It took me a long time just to realize that. But if it wasn't my fault,

52   Thirteen Things You Gotta Know

then why do I have to do *anything*? Why can't God just take it away from me?"

Sometimes Liz and Darcelle would answer her, and sometimes they would just listen in silence.

As Christmas approached, Joy's usual anticipation and excitement were blocked. Bitterness rose in her at the thought of another Christmas with her family: the smiles, the photographs, the carols, the presents, the prayers—it all seemed hollow and hypocritical.

She'd run away before, but that was before she became a Christian. On the other hand, she was much younger then; she could probably get away this time. *Maybe they'd stop and think— for once—how much they hurt me*, she thought. *To run away on Christmas Day. . . .* Something in the idea appealed to her.

Christmas Eve she packed a tiny suitcase and slid it under her bed. A confused excitement filled her as she drifted off to sleep, imagining her parents' shocked expressions when they came in to wake her up and she wasn't there.

Joy tiptoed downstairs with her case in hand early Christmas morning. She ate a leisurely breakfast of toast and cereal before her parents awoke. Heavy footsteps and running water upstairs signalled that her father was awake. She spooned the rest of the cereal into her mouth, placed her bowl in the kitchen sink and put the box back in the cupboard next to the sink. In the cupboard was a box of Pop Tarts. Taking two packages from the box and slipping them in her purse, she glanced around the kitchen one last time. She was about to wipe the crumbs and spot of milk from the table, but changed her mind. She inhaled deeply, gripped the suitcase handle, and stepped to the kitchen door, pausing with her other hand on the door handle.

The hurt is still there, Joy. It's trapped deep down in you, and you won't get it out until you stop running from it. Liz's words returned to her mind.

"I'm not running from my hurt," she muttered. "I'm running from *them*."

The sound of running water stopped. She listened to the sound of closet doors and dresser drawers opening and closing, and soon after, the steps began to creak. She clutched the doorknob tighter.

It's trapped . . .

The third step from the bottom, the one that creaked the loudest in the old house, announced her father's descent to the bottom of the staircase.

Stop running . . .

Joy jerked the door open and slid through, snagging her shirt on the screen door handle. She freed herself quickly, then gently pushed the screen door shut against the pressure of the closing mechanism. She stole to the edge of the porch, jumped over the steps, and hid around the corner, waiting for the door to open and her father to emerge after her.

She backed against her house, trying to control her breathing.

You won't get it out . . .

"I'm not running," she said again. No one came out of the door. She heard movement in the kitchen. "I may not be confronting my hurt, but I'm *not* running."

The hurt is still there, Joy.

"I still can't do it," Joy said, not sure whether she was talking to Liz or to God. "I can't."

"Joy?" From inside the house—probably the foot of the steps—came the distant sound of her mother's voice.

She sighed deeply. "I don't know if I can do it, Lord. I can try, but I don't know if I can do it."

She left her case and her purse on the ground beside the house and climbed the steps. "Lord," she prayed as she opened the door, "I'm going to try to say it. Help me to mean it."

PowerLink   PowerThink

A new Christian often has a sensation of being refreshingly clean and free upon first experiencing God's forgiveness. Often, however, a surprise awaits him when he realizes that forgiveness of sins is not necessarily the same thing as healing of hurts.

As Liz explained to Joy, "God forgives you for things *you* have done, for sins *you* have committed." Sometimes, however, things still hurt because you don't need *forgiveness*; you need *healing*.

- Read page 143 of *Under Siege*, where Joy shares her testimony of what happened that Christmas Day when she confronted her parents and told them she forgave them.

  Joy's parents got angry and did not accept her forgiveness. What effect do you think that would have on the healing process she desired? Would it make a difference? Would it help her to heal? Prevent her? Or neither?

- God deals with our hurts in a variety of ways. 1 Peter 5:7 tells us, "Give all your worries to [God], because he cares for you." The word "worries" in that verse can include painful memories. Does this mean that God heals some (or all) hurts and anxieties with a wave of His hand? What does it mean to give your worries to God?

- Read Luke 22:54–62, which describes an incident involving Peter and Jesus. How do you think this incident affected Jesus? Why do you think Luke included his comment in verse 61, "Then the Lord turned and looked straight at Peter"?

- *Now* read John 21:15–19, in which Jesus communicates forgiveness to Peter. What also might be happening in these verses? Could Jesus be confronting the hurt that Peter caused Him?

- Notice how gently and patiently Jesus confronts Peter. It wasn't a shouting match, was it? What does that teach you today about confronting your hurts?

- Are there hurts in your life that need healing? Take a pencil and paper and make a prayer list for healing. First, cast all those hurts on God; commit them to Him. Then, determine which of those hurts may require action from you for healing to take place. (Is there someone you need to forgive, something you need to release?) Finally, while you take action as necessary, continue praying and waiting expectantly for God to answer your prayers.

Copy Psalm 147:3 below:

- Conclude your time of devotion today with the following prayer of praise:

  Praise be to the God and Father of our Lord Jesus Christ. God is the Father who is full of mercy. And he is the God of all comfort.[4]

---

4. 2 Corinthians 1:3

Lord, please let me feel Your mercy and comfort very close to me as I commit all my hurts to You and wait for Your healing. Amen.

- Day 2   Read 2 Corinthians 4:7–12 and follow with prayer:

Father, sometimes I feel that way. I have troubles all around me. I hurt sometimes. Please help me, though, like Paul, not to be destroyed or defeated, but to know Christ's life working a new life in me. Amen.

- Day 3   Read 2 Corinthians 4:13–18. Now read it again, in prayer, praising God for the blessings mentioned in those verses.

- Day 4   Read 2 Corinthians 5:1–7. Now pray those verses, inserting the pronouns "I," "me," and "my" for "We," "us," and "ours."

- Day 5   Read 2 Corinthians 5:8–15. Spend a few moments praising God before presenting your requests to Him.

- Day 6   Read 2 Corinthians 5:16–20. Close by praying:

Father, help me to realize that, in Christ, I am a new creature; the old things have gone; everything is made new. Help me to live in that newness and shed the hurts and pains of the past. Amen.

- Day 7   Read Jude 24–25. After a few moments of personal prayer, close with:

I read these verses not long ago, Father. Today I pray them to praise You that glory, greatness, power, and authority belong to You through Jesus Christ my Lord for all time past, *now and forever. Amen.*

*But God's grace has made me what I am,
and his grace to me was not wasted.*

1 Corinthians 15:10

6

Krystal's Worth

Krystal shuddered as she removed the empty condom package from under her bed left there from last week. She scanned her room quickly, though she knew no one was watching her. She carefully placed the wrapper between other items in her wastebasket.

Krystal had been a Christian for a couple of days now, and her life had already changed drastically. She had been one of the most successful drug pushers at Eisenhower High, selling drugs she obtained (and sometimes stole) from her own father. She had also been a user herself, and had occasionally frightened herself with her increasing tolerance and dependence on several kinds of drugs. And occasionally, when her habit consumed more money than her dealing brought in, she would sell herself.

It's not like it's with total strangers, she remembers telling herself. *It's only with boys I know, and I always use protection. And there are some boys I would never sleep with—so it's not the same as being a prostitute.*

She used to think that having someone pay for her ought to make a girl feel good; people only pay for something of value, right? But it had the opposite effect, increasing the sense of worthlessness she'd had, it seemed, all her life.

Now, as she cleaned her room, preparing to move out of her parents' house and in with her friend Darcelle, reminders of her past flooded her with an awareness of her shortcomings.

She sat down on the edge of her bed. "I know I've said this before, Lord, but I'm really sorry for all the things I've done. I know You've forgiven me, but I know I don't deserve it, either. I could never measure up to my own sister, never mind trying to live up to—"

A knock on her door broke her reverie and a moment later, Darcelle entered.

"Oh, I think I've just about got it done," she answered when Darcelle offered to help. "I was just sitting here thinking . . ."

Darcelle sat on the bed next to her.

"You look pretty low," Darcelle said.

"Yeah. I'll be okay." Krystal avoided Darcelle's eyes and moved briskly about her room in silence, finishing her packing and cleaning.

"Your parents aren't home?" Darcelle asked as she helped Krystal load her things into the car.

"No," Krystal said flatly.

The rest of the loading, driving, and unloading took place in silence.

"I'm going out," Krystal told Darcelle as she slipped out the door, leaving the boxes stacked in her new room at Darcelle's house.

Krystal walked the short distance to the mall, where she supposed some of her old friends would be hanging out.

She entered at the door nearest the Dark Castle Arcade and immediately ran into Nicole, one of her closest friends before she came to Christ. The two stood between the arcade and the Cookie Corner, talking and laughing. Krystal's depression began to lift.

Two boys and a girl approached them, and Nicole nudged Krystal with an elbow. Krystal stood aside as Nicole approached them and, with frequent sly glances around her, pulled some plastic bags out of her pockets. Nicole motioned for Krystal to come closer, but Krystal remained rooted to the floor where she stood.

"What's wrong with you?" Nicole asked when she had completed the sale and returned to Krystal's side. "Why didn't you come over?"

Krystal shrugged.

"Is it true what Julie said, that you're some kind of religious weirdo now?"

"I don't—" Krystal began.

"I mean, she said you don't party anymore. Is that true?" Nicole stopped only for a moment, then went on, "And you don't use *or* party? What's wrong with you, Krystal? You used to be so much fun." Nicole continued her nonstop badgering until Krystal turned and began to walk away without a word. "We used to have a blast together, but now you're a—" Nicole shouted some profane names at Krystal's retreating form.

Krystal returned to Darcelle's house, stomped in the door and ran up to her room.

Her door had hardly closed behind her when Darcelle knocked.

"Are you okay?" she asked, after Krystal had mumbled, "Come in."

Krystal didn't answer.

"I was worried about you." Darcelle sat cross-legged on the floor, near the apparent object of Krystal's vacant stare. She moved a box out of the way so she could lean against the wall. "There may not be much I can do, Krystal, but I can listen if you want to talk."

The two sat in silence again.

Krystal sat unmoving, staring, while Darcelle shifted uneasily.

"I feel like garbage," Krystal said, finally.

The two girls met each others' gaze.

"I thought maybe when I became a Christian that it would make me feel like I was worth something.

"See, ever since I can remember, I've felt worthless. I've never been as good as my sister Kathy, I could never please my dad, and I always seem to pick friends who are prettier or smarter than I am.

"If I could only be like you, Darcelle. When I'm around you, I think, *that's* what a Christian should be like. But I'm not like you or your mom or Liz. And then I go around my old friends and they make me feel like—"

Krystal's voice broke and her lip quivered.

"They make me feel like—"

She stopped again and began to cry.

Darcelle stood and left the room. Krystal only noticed her movement when she returned, carrying a dark blue Bible, to sit beside her on the bed.

"You *are* like me, Krystal," Darcelle said softly. Krystal blinked at her. "Well, you are, and you aren't.

"Hold on a minute, and I'll explain." She flipped her Bible open. "From the very beginning, the Bible says that you're made in the image of God. Look here." Darcelle moved her Bible onto Krystal's lap. "Genesis 1:26. No, let's read verse 27. 'So God created human beings in his own image. In the image of God he created them. He created them male and female.' What does that say about you?"

Krystal gazed at the page for a moment before answering, dully, "I'm created in the image of God."

"Right."

"Yeah, but so is everybody else in the world."

"Right. So?"

"Well, that doesn't make me special."

"Yes it does. You're not the only person in the world who's special, but you *are* special, because God created you in His own image. Let me show you something else."

Darcelle turned a pile of pages over in her Bible and then fanned through a few more. "This is neat. My mom showed me this once." She flipped one more thin page and pointed to a verse. "Ephesians 2:10. 'God has made us what we are. In Christ Jesus, God made us new people so that we would do good works. God had planned in advance those good works for us. He had planned for us to live our lives doing them.'

"So you're not only special because God created you—like He did everybody in the world—but you're special because He created you all over again a couple of days ago. He has made you what you are, Krystal. It's like being a great masterpiece hanging in some museum—the Master made you! You're a work of art."

"I don't feel like a work of art."

"Yeah, sometimes I don't either. But learning to like myself has been kind of a long process for me. I've been a Christian for a few years, Krystal, not a few days like you have, but I'm still learning that, like those posters say, 'God don't make no junk.'

"And think about this, too: God paid the highest price for you, when He sent Jesus to die on the cross. That's gotta say something about what you're worth."

Krystal's back straightened and her jaw tightened. She remembered her former life, how she used to think that having guys pay to be with her should make her feel worth something—but it never did. *Because I was worth way more than that; I just never realized it,* she thought. *God gave His Son for me. He paid the highest price there is—for me! That's how much I'm worth to Him.*

Krystal peered at Darcelle through the tears that were forming in her eyes. She wrapped her arms around her friend and squeezed.

"Thank you," she whispered.

"Just remember," Darcelle said as she hugged Krystal back, "you'll still have bad days, days when you don't feel like a work of art. Just memorize that verse and keep reminding yourself, 'God has made me what I am.' Okay?"

Krystal answered by tightening her grip until Darcelle let out a gasp as if she were being strangled. The girls laughed in each other's arms.

PowerLink   PowerThink

Why is it so hard for people—young people especially—to like themselves? One reason may be because God created us to love and obey Him; and when a person is not doing that, he or she will be unfulfilled and feel incomplete.

Why is a healthy sense of self-esteem so rare even among Christians? Perhaps it's because the devil knows that if he can convince you that you're worthless, it will be easier to defeat you as a Christian. But if, on the other hand, you realize how much you're worth to God, you'll find it easier to live victoriously.

Explore in thought, word, and deed the path to a healthy Christian sense of your self-worth.

- Record producer Michael Omartian says, "It was easy for me to equate personal security and well-being with success. I heard it every day of my life: 'Be successful, powerful, and rich and be happy and fulfilled.' What a lie! Jesus came to fulfill us at our deepest level, freeing us from the need to be successful to feel we are worthwhile, and freeing us from feeling worthless when failures come."

- Ask yourself, "Am I free from the need to be successful to feel worthwhile?" Ask yourself, "Am I free from feeling worthless when failures come?" If the answer to either question is no, what can you do to change that?

- Read Genesis 1:27. What do you think it means to be made "in the image of God"? Does it mean you look like Him? Something else? Take some time to ponder the fact that you are made in God's image.

- Read Ephesians 2:10. Notice the first phrase—"God has made us what we are." Say it out loud to yourself, rephrasing it: "God has made *me* what I am." That seems a rather obvious statement; why do you think Paul said that?

- When Paul wrote that verse, he wrote it in the Greek language and used an interesting word. In effect, he wrote, "God has made us *poiema*," a word that referred to explicitly creative works of art. In fact, *poiema* is the root of our word "poem." In other words, Paul said that *you* are God's "poem," God's "sculpture," God's "symphony," God's "masterpiece"—like Darcelle told Krystal—God's "work of art." Which description do you think fits you best? Why?

- List below the three things you like most about yourself (don't be modest):

Take a few moments in prayer to thank God for those things.

- List the three things that make it hardest for you to like yourself (don't be afraid to be honest):

Take a few moments in prayer to ask God's help in overcoming those things.

- Look up 1 Corinthians 15:10 and copy the first half of the verse below. Use this as your motto for the week:

- Call your local Christian radio station and request the song, "We Are the Reason" by David Meece (or buy or listen to it at a Christian book and tape store). Listen closely to it; how do you react to the song?

- Day 2   Read Matthew 6:26 and 10:28–31 and follow with prayer:

    Father, I know that not one little bird can die without You knowing it. Help me also to know that I am worth much more than many birds to You. Give me assurance today of Your care and love for me. Amen.

- Day 3   Read 1 Corinthians 6:19–20. Do you know that you're the temple of God? Do you know you were bought with a price? What price did God pay to redeem you? Spend some time in prayer, thanking God for His costly redemption.

- Day 4   Read Ephesians 3:20–21. Now read those verses again, inserting the pronouns "me," "I" for "us" and "we." Close with prayer.

- Day 5   Read Psalm 8:4–6. Spend a few moments thanking God that He thinks so highly of you before presenting your requests to Him.

- Day 6   Read Psalm 139:13–16. Spend some time thanking God for creating you as His "masterpiece"; then present your requests to Him.

• Day 7   Read Revelation 1:4–6. Who is "the One who loves us," who made us "free from our sins"? What did He make us to be? Close by praying:

Father, help me to truly believe in my heart that I am loved by You. Help me to realize that You've also made me to be part of a kingdom of priests who serve You. Help me to live in the knowledge that You think I'm priceless. Amen.

Confess your sins to each other and pray for each other so God can heal you.

James 5:16

7

Jason's Problem

Jason snatched the remote and flipped the channel.

He craned his neck behind him, but couldn't see anyone. He pointed the remote at the set again, turned the volume all the way down and listened.

After a few moments of silence, he let out a quiet, but deep, sigh. "Thought I heard something," he whispered. After another look toward the bedrooms he turned the volume up, but softer than it was before, and switched back to the X-rated cable movie he'd been watching.

Jason's parents were gone for the weekend and his best friend, Will McConnell, was staying over while his mother was at a marketing seminar. The two had ordered pizza, watched television, even talked and prayed about the Liberation Commandos and their efforts to witness to their friends. Finally, a little after midnight, the two went to bed.

Jason had not gone to sleep, however. He had waited quietly until Will's tossing stopped and his breathing slowed. Then he crept out of the room and down the hall, plopped onto the couch, turned the television on, and pressed the familiar numbers of *The Adult Channel* on the remote.

Finally, after one movie and half of another, he switched the set off and returned to his room. He lay awake on his sleeping bag, while Will slept on the bed beside him. His friend's presence made him uncomfortable.

That was pretty stupid, Withers, Jason thought, his eyes wide open. *What if Will had gotten up to go to the bathroom or something? What if your best friend knew you watched that kind of stuff?*

Jason was overwhelmed with a sense of guilt and shame.

God, he prayed, mouthing the words in the dark room, *I'm really sorry. I know it's a filthy habit I have, but I can't do anything about it. I can go five or six days real good, but I always end up giving in when I'm home alone.*

It scared him that this time he'd watched that channel when Will was in the house. *If Will ever found out. . . .*

God, I know Satan really wants to mess up what we've been doing in the Liberation Commandos.

He rolled onto his side in mid-prayer, and for a few moments, his thoughts became disjointed. He thought about the movie, about Will, about his parents. A dozen other thoughts and images passed through his brain until he remembered that he had been praying. *Please help me,* he continued, *please help me resist the devil and find a way to keep from sinning.*

He closed his eyes. In the last moments before he drifted to sleep, he decided, *I'm going to talk to Will about it in the morning. I'll find a way to get it out in the open and he'll help me never do it again.*

The day passed quickly, and Jason said nothing to Will about the night before. He found, in fact, that he could barely meet his friend's eyes, and he felt awkward in his presence, as if Will already knew his dirty secret.

Three or four times, Jason wavered between thinking he would tell Will and feeling he could never make such a confession. They spent time together as they always had, but Jason constantly wrestled with the secret he was keeping from his friend, and it seemed to make their times together awkward and tense.

"Jason," Will said a couple days later when they were alone again. His tone caused a knot to form in Jason's stomach. "I need to ask your help with something."

Jason breathed an inward sigh of relief.

"I, uh . . . ahem." Will cleared his throat half-heartedly, and proceeded to tell Jason a little of the struggles he'd been having with fantasies about Amber. He told him he needed his prayers and asked him if it was all right for him to call Jason when he needed support.

Jason smiled. "Sure, Will," he said, and then both lapsed into silence. Jason felt as if he had narrowly escaped a catastrophe; Will clicked his fingernails nervously, hoping and praying that Jason would take this opportunity to confess. Jason didn't know that Will had seen him watching that movie in the family room, but had gone back to bed without saying a word.

This would be a good time to tell him, Jason thought. But his tongue seemed lodged way down in his chest, and even as he thought it, he knew he wouldn't confide in Will.

"Jason," Will started. "I saw you watching that movie the other night."

The back of Jason's neck and the tops of his ears began to burn. He suddenly felt shaky inside.

"I thought maybe we could talk about it," Will said after a moment of painful silence.

"What were you doing, spying on me?" Jason snapped. "I can't believe you'd do that to your best friend."

Jason felt a sickening mixture of anger, embarrassment and fear. He snarled at his friend, and told him that it was none of his business, that he couldn't sleep, that he just happened to turn to that channel and "if you'd said something, you'd have found out that I was really watching something else." He talked loudly for a few minutes, never meeting Will's eyes. Finally, he stopped, and after a long time in which neither spoke, Jason looked at Will.

In the moment they looked at each other, Jason felt his anger wane. Another long silence followed. Jason gazed at the ground until he gathered the guts to begin talking. In a completely different, quiet voice, he confessed to Will that he'd had this problem for a long time. He admitted that he couldn't seem to resist the temptation; whenever he was home alone—which, with his parents' schedules, was often—he couldn't keep from watching the stuff.

Jason's eyes teared up and, as he was telling these things to his friend, his voice choked.

After Jason's confession, Will suggested they pray together.

Will committed to pray for Jason every day and to hold him accountable—all in strictest confidence. Jason promised to do the same for Will in his struggles with temptation.

Over the course of the next couple of weeks, the two occasionally talked about their promises, and prayed together a few times. The first time Jason's parents left him alone after the confrontation, he called Will and they prayed over the phone. Will offered to come over, but Jason promised instead that at the first sign of weakness, he'd come over to Will's. The night passed almost without a struggle.

Two days later, however, when his parents were out again, Jason turned to *The Adult Channel* without so much as a thought of his agreement with Will. He became engrossed in the events on the screen; they filled his mind so completely that only on waking the next morning was he stricken with the guilt of his sin.

God, I blew it. That didn't take very long, did it? At least I didn't mess up the first *chance I got.*

He remembered his promise to Will. *I'm supposed to tell Will, I guess. But what good would that do? I can understand calling him when I need him to pray or help me before I do it, but what can he do now? It's already done. It'll just make us both feel bad; I'll feel embarrassed and he'll think I'm a jerk. I'll just make sure that next time I do better.*

Jason felt a little uneasy, but he was fully determined not to fail again as he had the night before. *As long as I don't do it again,* he reasoned, *there's no need to tell Will.* He felt a nagging reminder in his brain that he was keeping secrets again, but he dismissed it quickly.

He caught himself every once in awhile planning or guessing the next time his parents would be gone, leaving him alone. He told himself that he was only trying to foresee the temptation, but such thoughts were combined with mental pictures of himself on the family room couch and pornographic images on the television screen.

When the phone rang, Jason immediately hoped it was his father or mother telling him of another business trip, and he also knew the reason for that hope.

It was Will.

Jason's disappointment combined with a fearful feeling in his stomach, the same feeling he used to get as a child when he played with matches in his closet. He knew he was getting very close to a disastrous mistake.

Will was full of news about something-or-other, but Jason heard little of what he said.

He's in such a good mood, Jason thought. *I'll just bring him down if I tell him about last night.*

Will prattled on.

I can't just butt in and change the subject.

Jason felt a cough rising in his throat. He stifled it, but it still escaped as a weak, airy sound.

"What?" Will stopped in mid-sentence.

"Huh?" Jason hadn't even been listening.

"Were you going to say something?" Will asked.

"Oh," Jason said, and a feeling of urgency assailed him. *It's now or never. Well? What's it gonna be?* He opened his mouth to say no, but at the last second he jumped in the same way he entered a swimming pool filled with cold water: all at once.

"Yeah," he said, "I've got something to tell you."

Jason went on to tell Will about the night before, how he had turned on the television almost automatically, and had given in to the sin without so much as a struggle. He went on to tell him how he'd almost talked himself out of confessing to Will, how up until that very moment, he'd been dodging the agreement they'd made together.

"I am *so* glad you told me all this," Will said when Jason was through. He told Jason how he was afraid they'd both kind of back out of the agreement, and now he felt more confidence in their friendship than ever before. "It shows how much we've grown in our relationship with the Lord, Jason," he said. "Six months ago, we could never have been this honest with each other."

"You're not mad, then?"

"No. I'm not saying I'm glad you gave in to the temptation, but, man, I *am* glad you trust me enough to tell me."

"Yeah," Jason said in a pleased tone. "Yeah, that's pretty great, isn't it? You know what, Will?"

"What?"

"You're more than just a pretty face."

The two laughed with each other over the phone, then prayed, then laughed some more.

==

PowerLink   PowerThink

Will and Jason stumbled onto a crucial ingredient in living the Christian life: accountability.

Accountability is just a six-syllable word for having someone who supports and corrects you when it's necessary.

A student is accountable to his teacher; the teacher makes assignments, grades them, and offers congratulations or detention as necessary!

An athlete is accountable to her coach. "Have you been doing your wind sprints lately?" "I notice you're dropping your elbow on your swing."

A new Christian needs to be accountable to another Christian, a mature Christian, someone who can support and correct you. Finding someone to be accountable to is a major step in assuring growth and victory in your Christian life.

- What do you think would have happened if Jason had *not* told Will of his failure?

- Aren't your sins something that are best kept between you and God? What would be the value of telling someone else about your failures and successes?

- Read James 5:16. Two ingredients of a successful partnership, such as Will and Jason had, are mentioned in this verse. What are they? Write them below:

- James then says, "Do this so that God can heal you. When a good man prays, great things happen." What do those two statements have to do with confessing your sins to each other and praying for each other?

- Notice in that verse the repetition of the phrase "each other." Are those words important? Why or why not?

- Take a few moments to think about your friends. Then consider if any of them possess the following characteristics that might recommend him or her to be the kind of person who could hold you accountable:

   A mature Christian. Two new Christians can be a source of enormous encouragement to each other, but seek a mature Christian who can not only listen, but also share with you some of what he or she has learned from successes and failures.

   Someone you trust. Your "confession and prayer partner" must also be someone you can trust with your darkest secrets, as well as someone who will trust you. Remember that Will helped Jason open up about his problem by confiding some of his own struggles. You also must be able to feel certain that your partner will keep all the confidences you share.

Someone of the same gender. Some of your closest friends are probably members of the opposite sex; we recommend, however, that guys seek a male partner and girls seek a female partner. As with Jason and Will, this could prove a valuable advantage in helping you to be honest and understanding with each other, and could also prevent distractions or difficulties in the future.

Someone nearby. You might want to enter into a covenant with your best friend who moved to Minnesota last year, but consider someone nearby, who can meet you at McDonald's or read the expressions on your face instead of only reading letters or listening to your voice over the telephone. It's ideal to have a partner whom you see nearly everyday.

Does anyone among your closest circle of friends or respected adults come to mind as a potential partner? If not, pray this prayer:

> *Father, I thank You for showing me the benefit of having someone to confess to and pray with, someone who will help keep me honest before You. Please guide me to the person You've chosen to be my friend and confidante. In Jesus' name, Amen.*

• If you have thought of someone who might make a helpful "confession and prayer partner," pray this prayer, inserting that person's name in the blanks:

> *Father, I thank You that I have among my friends someone like_____. I pray that you'll help me to approach _____ soon about entering into an agreement with me, to confess our sins to each other,*

pray for each other, and hold each other accountable. I pray, too, that you'll prepare _____ to respond according to Your will when I ask. Make our friendship a means for us both to live growing, victorious Christian lives. In Jesus' name, Amen.

- Day 2   Read Matthew 18:15–17. Pray for your prayer partner or prospective partner, inserting his or her name in the blank:

  Father, help me to understand and obey your Word. Make me Your loving child and _____'s caring Christian brother/sister. Amen.

- Day 3   Read Matthew 18:18–20. Pray for your personal needs and desires.

- Day 4   Read Mark 6:7–13. Why do you think Jesus sent the disciples out "in groups of two?" Pray for your family.

- Day 5   Read Luke 10:1–3. Notice the phrase "in pairs." Any new ideas as to why Jesus paired His followers? Pray today for your closest circle of friends.

- Day 6   Read Acts 13:1–3. Thank God for bringing godly friends into your life.

- Day 7   Read Ephesians 3:14–21. Pray these verses, first for yourself (inserting "I," "me," and "my"), then for your family and friends (inserting "they," "them," and "their").

Ask, and God will give to you. Search, and you will find. Knock, and the door will open for you.

Matthew 7:7

8

Reggie's Idea

"Why do I even bother?"

Reggie Spencer slammed the kitchen phone into its cradle.

"Forget you, Mom," he said through gritted teeth. He stomped to the family room and popped a football bloopers tape into the VCR, then sprawled on the couch and ignored the action on the screen.

"I can't believe her," he said, and fell silent for a few moments, while mental pictures of his mother and her seemingly endless parade of men marched through his mind. She hadn't come home again last night, and had called a few minutes ago to "see if everything was all right."

"Yeah, Mom, you can just—" He checked his tongue in time, but the profanity that almost came out reflected his deep anger.

Reggie was still a new Christian. A few days after he went with the Westcastle Community Church youth group on a campout to Gilligan's Lake, the new youth leader, Duane Cunningham, had invited him for lunch at McDonald's. Reggie had been stirred by something at the campout, but didn't respond until Duane sat across the table from him, explaining God's love and Jesus' sacrifice for his sins. When Duane urged him, Reggie bowed his head over the remains of his lunch, and surrendered his life to Christ.

Reggie had told the story of his coming to Christ at the next youth meeting at Duane's apartment. A burst of applause erupted after his testimony. A few kids even jumped up to hug Reggie or shake his hand.

Then Krystal had told her story, explaining that Liz had met with her the same night and helped her trust Christ. Krystal also received a hero's salute.

After Reggie and Krystal sat down, Duane asked, "How many of you remember receiving an invitation to be part of a new prayer team for our group?" Almost everyone raised a hand. "Well, a few of us have been meeting every week to pray for our youth group. Tonight you have seen what God can do when kids pray."

Duane's comment stuck with Reggie: "Tonight you have seen what God can do when kids pray." He made it sound so · powerful, so impressive.

But since that night, Reggie's ideas about prayer had suffered major blows, and his mother's behavior only made things worse.

He got up from the couch, leaving the VCR to play football follies to an empty room, and returned to the phone.

"Hi, Duane," he said flatly after Liz had called her husband to the phone.

"Yeah, I guess I am," he said in answer to Duane's observation that he sounded kind of depressed. "It's Mom again."

Reggie paused before responding to Duane's next statement.

"She didn't come home again last night."

He stretched for a kitchen chair, just out of reach.

"Hold on a minute, Duane."

Reggie held the phone at arm's length and pulled the chair over.

"Okay."

He listened to Duane repeat what he had said earlier.

"Yeah, I guess," he said hesitantly.

"It's just," he started before Duane finished, "it's just praying's not doing any good. I mean—"

He let Duane interrupt and listened.

"Yeah, I've prayed like crazy," he said, saying the last word like someone had squeezed it out of him.

"Yeah," he answered Duane.

"At *least* every day," he answered again, then listened another moment.

"For a few weeks," he said.

Reggie took a deep breath.

"Nothing's changed with my mom *or* my dad."

He twisted the phone cord around his foot.

"No, but God hasn't answered *any* of my prayers."

He paused.

"Hardly any."

He paused again.

"I don't see—"

Another pause.

"Yeah, I guess I could do that."

Then, after a moment, "No, that's okay. I've got something I can use."

Reggie hung up the phone, stared at the receiver for a minute, then trudged upstairs to his room.

He fished around in his desk drawer until he found an old spiral notebook. He flipped through it quickly, tore out the first few pages, and sat down to write.

He began listing the things he'd been praying for since he'd become a Christian, leaving space to record times he prayed for them from now on and an extra column labeled "ANSWERS."

Remembering something Duane had said a few moments before on the phone, Reggie snapped his fingers and added an entry at the top of the list: "Prayed for salvation." He dated the prayer and the answer identically.

Over the course of the next two weeks, Reggie discovered that his prayer times were not only getting longer, but he was also starting to pray more specific things; instead of praying for God to "bless so-and-so," he would pray for God to begin to convict his mother of her sin, and help Tony Ortiz to see something in his changed life that would make him think about spiritual things.

He began to realize that prayer isn't like requesting a song on a radio station, but more like developing a friendship. Some things about a new friend may puzzle you at first, but as you get closer to your friend, you begin to know how your friend thinks, what your friend likes, and why your friend acts certain ways.

As he compiled and added to his list, Reggie realized that he'd been concentrating so much on the prayers God hadn't yet answered, he'd overlooked some that were answered quickly—even immediately, like his prayer for salvation.

The more he prayed, the more he understood prayer.

The more he prayed, the more he enjoyed it.

The more he prayed, the more results he saw, until he began to believe in the power of prayer.

That's why Reggie Spencer had come up with the idea at the Commandos' meeting the Thursday before Thanksgiving.

"You remember that 'See You at the Pole' thing back in September?" he said. "Where a bunch of us Christian kids at school gathered around the flagpole for prayer and a visible witness? Maybe the eight of us together should do something like that again."

At first the group applauded Reggie's idea. But then they couldn't decide how to do it, and soon they were bickering about when to do it. "Hey, wait a minute!" Duane interrupted as the normally cohesive Commandos snipped at each other. "It sounds like we're getting increased resistance from the enemy. Let's stop and pray right now that God's plan won't be foiled by our selfishness or Satan's interference."

The Commandos sheepishly admitted that Duane was right, and a few apologies were exchanged. Then Duane led the group in prayer. "Lord, we know from the resistance we have experienced tonight that our prayer sorties are taking a toll on the enemy. We stand against our pride and selfishness and the distractions around us. We resist the enemy's attempts to place us under siege and keep us from completing our mission. Keep leading us into victory as we work with You in Your rescue mission."

The rest of the Liberation Commandos joined Duane in a hearty "amen." Then they quickly made plans for a "prayer walk" around the school ending with a "prayer stand" at the flagpole during lunch period on the day before Thanksgiving.

PowerLink   PowerThink

Does your understanding of prayer come from your child-hood, from listening to grown-ups talk to God in thee's and thou's or six-syllable theological words you'd never heard of?

Relax. Prayer is simply talking to God about your thoughts, feelings and concerns. And God really does understand mod-ern English (even the bizarre language spoken by teenagers). And you can be totally confident that God hears you when you pray. In fact, God eagerly waits for you to come to Him in prayer. You are His child, and He values every minute you spend with Him!

Why is prayer so great? Here are some important answers.

1. Prayer helps us focus on God. It puts our eyes on God and helps us know Him better. The psalmist said, "Look to the Lord and his strength; seek his face always" (Psalm 105:4). When we take time to pray, we "unplug" our minds from the television and the CD player, and "plug in" to God.

2. Prayer is intimacy with God. When you pray, you discover what it means to be intimate with God. The Bible says that when Moses entered the tabernacle, "The Lord would speak with Moses face to face, as a man speaks with his friend" (Exodus 33:11). *That* is what happens in prayer. You become friends with God. You develop more than an acquaintance with Him; He becomes a deep, intimate, personal friend who loves you unconditionally. As you relate to God in prayer, you will stay in tune with His heartbeat for you and the captives around you.

3. Prayer is a vital weapon in spiritual battle. We have seen from Will and Amber's lives that spiritual conflict is a reality. We face it every day. And prayer is the "big gun" in our spiritual arsenal.

In Ephesians 6:10–20, Paul lists the armor we are to use in fighting the spiritual battle. He says we are to wear our faith as a shield against Satan's flaming arrows, put on the helmet of salvation, and use the sword of the Spirit which is God's Word (verses 16–17).

Then Paul lists prayer, not once but four times, as it applies to spiritual warfare. He says, "Pray in the Spirit on all occasions with all kinds of prayers. . . . Be alert and always keep on praying for all the saints [Christians]. Pray also for me . . . so that I will fearlessly make known the mystery of the gospel. . . . Pray that I may declare it fearlessly as I should" (verses 18–20).

When we pray, God takes action! Your prayers for your non-Christian friends paralyze Satan as God works in their lives. He prepares your friends to receive the message that He gives you the strength to share.

- What is the last answer to prayer that you recall? What is the last prayer of yours that God *didn't* answer? What was the difference?

- How do you remember what you've prayed? Do you tend to remember unanswered prayers more than answered prayers?

- Read the following Scripture verses carefully and prayer-fully. Then, in the space provided, indicate whether the verse contains a command, a promise, or an instruction regarding prayer (some verses contain more than one).

Matthew 7:7 _instruction + promise_

John 16:24 _command promise_

Ephesians 6:18 _command, instruction_

Philippians 4:6 _command instruction_

Colossians 4:2–4 _Command, instruction_

- Now, consider those verses again and ask, "Am I obeying the command? Have I claimed the promise? What can I learn from the instruction?"

- You may think about how wonderful it will be when your non-Christian friends trust Christ. But thinking nice thoughts isn't the same as praying. Prayer is an action. Prayer is taking time to talk to God specifically about what you're thinking. Here are some ways to become an active pray-er:

Go to God regularly to pray. Begin by thanking and praising Him for His greatness.

Pray alone over your personal list of non-Christian friends.

Pray regularly for non-Christians with a small group of friends.

Take time in your church or Christian student meeting to pray together about your witness to non-Christians.

Join with other Christians at school for a prayer walk around or through your campus. We're not talking about a noisy, showy religious procession. Just get together to walk around the areas where kids congregate: cafeteria, auditorium, classrooms, bleachers. As you walk, pray silently for God's power to be released so that many captives may be released and trust Christ.

Prayer is the big gun, the ultimate spiritual weapon. As you pray, God prepares you to do what He has called you to do.

* Day 2   Read Luke 18:1–8. Spend some time praising God for who He is, thanking Him for what He's done, and telling Him the desires of your heart.

* Day 3   Read John 14:12–13. Open your prayer time:

    Father, I praise you for the promise of answered prayer. Help me really to pray in Your name, according to Your will. Amen.

    Follow this by presenting your requests to God.

* Day 4   Read John 15:1–8. Pray for help "remaining" in Christ; pray for help following His teachings.

* Day 5   Read James 1:2–8. After prayers of praise to God, ask Him for wisdom in praying. Then pray for your family, friends, and your own personal needs.

* Day 6   Read James 5:13–18. Are you having troubles today? Pray. Are you happy? Sing praises.

• Day 7   Read 1 John 5:13–15. Conclude your prayer time:

> *Father, I come to You today with no doubts. May the*
> *things I've asked of You agree with what You want for*
> *me. Thank You for listening to what I say. Amen.*

Using the Scriptures, the person who serves God will be capable, having all that is needed to do every good work.

2 Timothy 3:17

9

Darcelle's Strength

Darcelle Davis wiped marble-sized tears from her face as she stood, embracing two other girls, in front of the nature lodge. They didn't notice the bread truck creeping toward them until the driver tapped the horn lightly.

The girls snorted and sniffed and smiled at the man in the truck as they stepped from the middle of the road.

"Oh, Neesy, I can't believe it's over," Darcelle cried, using her pet name for her friend Denise. Keila, the other girl, whimpered and shook her head.

"This—" Denise started, then sucked her lower lip in to stifle a sob before continuing. "This has been the best summer of my life. I wish it didn't have to end," she blurted. The trio huddled closer together. Then, as if on cue, Darcelle, Denise, and Keila straightened and began wiping their faces. Brad approached them.

"Excuse me ladies," he said through movie-star teeth. "But if you're going with me, Darcelle, it's time to leave." He shrugged apologetically, whirled, and walked back to his van.

Keila and Denise exchanged final hugs with Darcelle and posed identically to watch her run to the van: one arm folded across the chest, supporting the elbow of the other arm, which ended in a hand covering a quivering pair of lips.

After waving through the rear window at her friends until they disappeared behind the foliage that lined the camp road, Darcelle leaned back in the seat and shut her emotion-puffed eyes.

The first thoughts to fill her mind were expressions of thanks to God. This Christian camp had brought her to a radical commitment to Christ last summer, a few weeks before she started her freshman year in high school. This summer she had worked as a counselor, and besides becoming close friends with Denise and Keila, she had led a lot of kids to Christ and grown—unbelievably, she thought with a smile—in her own Christian life.

But the smile disappeared slowly as she remembered last year's experience. She had arrived home after the week-long conference, determined to read her Bible, pray every day, and do all the things she knew a Christian ought to do.

Yeah, she thought, her eyes still closed and the smile gone from her face. *How long did that last? A week, maybe?* She concentrated to remember what those first weeks home had been like. *No, two,* she allowed. *Two weeks, max. I started in the Gospel of John like everyone said I should. It was interesting, kinda neat,* she thought. *At first. But it wore off. I probably didn't even get through half the book,* she figured.

The van wheels hit a sizable bump and Darcelle opened her eyes as her head scuffed the roof.

"Sorry, Darcelle," said Brad. "Didn't see it coming." He smiled at her in the rear view mirror, and she slid down in her seat again.

I wonder if Brad struggles with this kind of thing, she thought. She considered asking him, but dismissed it quickly as she glanced at the pretty girl in the passenger seat beside Brad. *She'd think I was trying to flirt with him. I don't know why she's so jealous. If I looked like her. . .* Darcelle let the thought drop unfinished. She closed her eyes and leaned her head far back on the seat.

It's easy to see why I grew so much as a Christian this summer, she told herself. *It just seemed so natural—easy, almost—to read my Bible every day at camp. Some days I couldn't wait, it was like every day the thing I read in the Bible turned out to have some purpose, some meaning, or some thing that came true that same day. But it just doesn't work that way at home.*

It's not that Darcelle didn't try. She determined that it would be different this year, that she would continue the Bible reading and prayer, the growth that had started over the summer.

Before long, however, the thing she dreaded happened.

By the time school began, Darcelle's habit of Bible reading and study had disappeared; the thrill she had found in its pages evaporated; its relevance to her everyday life seemed to vanish. She was still a sincere Christian, but at times she felt that she was letting God down and putting on a show in front of her friends.

The priority of Bible study began to be replaced with other things in her life. She was a sophomore in high school now, and though her school, homework, clubs, and church activity filled her schedule, she craved more.

She'd spent weeks trying to persuade her mom to let her join the health club.

"Mercy, Darcelle, you already complain about having too much to do. I don't see how you're ever going to squeeze exercise classes into your schedule."

"But Mom," Darcelle pleaded, "I don't get the kind of exercise during the school year that I need. At camp it was easy, but I've already started putting weight back on since I've been home."

She informed her mother frequently as to how much weight she had gained. She dropped occasional hints about her clothes getting tight again. She even begged her mother—knowing all the time that she would refuse—to take nightly jogs with her.

Finally, after several weeks of continuous pressure, Darcelle won. Her mother took her to the club, signed papers, made the first monthly payment, and they each left the club with a photocopy of the club's schedule. Mrs. Davis shook her head.

"Darcelle, honey, I just don't know when you're going to do this."

"They have classes all the time, Mom. I just need to find the time that's best for me. I know it won't be easy, but it's important to me, so I'll make time for it."

"Mmmm hmm." Darcelle's mom shook her head again.

As Darcelle scanned the schedule later that evening, she began to get frustrated. The sessions that most interested her seemed all to be at the wrong times.

"If I get up forty-five minutes earlier on Mondays, Wednesdays and Fridays, I can go to Sweat Shop before school. Oh yeah, not Fridays; I have brass choir."

She turned the schedule over.

"It won't be easy. . . ." She squinted at the page. "Maybe Mom would let me—no, she'd never." Her index finger tapped the underside of the paper. Her eyes settled on the Aerobics session.

"Same time as newspaper meetings," she said. "Hmm. Tough choice." She hated to give that up. She seemed to hear her own voice: *I just need to find the time that's best for me. I know it won't be easy, but it's important to me, so I'll make time for it.*

"I'll have to think about that," she said, and set the schedule on her dresser next to her Bible, which had been so much a part of her summer experience. It had been days since she'd even tried to read or study it.

I just need to find the time that's best for me. I know it won't be easy, but it's important to me, so I'll make time for it.

She picked the book up tenderly and sat on the edge of her bed. She thumbed through its now-familiar pages. She heard her mother's voice,

Darcelle, honey, I just don't know when you're going to do this, then her own, *I just need to find the time that's best for me. I know it won't be easy, but it's important to me, so I'll make time for it.*

She flipped the pages.

John's Gospel. Finished it the first week of camp.

1 Corinthians 13. She had used that chapter several times for devotions with her campers.

Ephesians 6. She and Denise had presented an illustrated Scripture reading one Sunday night around the campfire, using pieces of armor they'd spent hours making in the craft lodge.

It was like every day the thing I read in the Bible turned out to have some purpose, some meaning, or some thing that came true that

same day, she remembered thinking. *But it just doesn't work that way at home.*

"Maybe that's because I don't read it at home," she muttered. She turned over more pages to 1 Timothy. She searched the headings in bold print and finally began reading under "Be a Good Servant of Christ." She read lazily until her brain was jerked to attention by the words of verse 8—she had to look again to notice that she was reading in chapter 4:

"Training your body helps you in some ways, but serving
God helps you in every way by bringing you blessings in
this life and in the future life, too."

She read it again. And a third time.

"I don't think I've ever read that verse before. Or if I did, it never hit me the way it does now." She blushed as she remembered her conversations with her mom. "The whole time I've been trying to squeeze this health club into my schedule I've been telling myself that I'm too busy to read my Bible."

I just need to find the time that's best for me. I know it won't be easy, but it's important to me, so I'll make time for it.

"It *is* important to me," she said. "And obviously God can make it come alive at home just as He does at camp. Maybe I need to get in shape physically, but I *know* I need to get in shape spiritually. And I'm going to start right now."

She reached a hand onto the dresser and crumpled the health club schedule. She drew a pencil and notebook from a desk drawer and sat down.

"If I get up forty-five minutes earlier. . . ."

===

PowerLink   PowerThink

Many young Christians find it difficult to read the Bible with any understanding, enjoyment, or satisfaction. Many know they *should* read it, even *want* to read it, but actually doing it seems next to impossible.

A regular habit of Bible reading and study can be hard work. Like physical exercise, it requires motivation, discipline, and perseverance. But like physical exercise, if reading God's Word is done regularly, the results will begin to show, and a day or two without spiritual exercise will leave you feeling sluggish and slow.

- Turn to page 14 in *Under Seige*. Darcelle Davis is described in the second and third paragraphs on that page; can you determine how much time passed between the events of the above chapter and the description of Darcelle in *Under Seige*?

- What might you be like a year from now if you were to begin a habit of daily prayer and Bible study right now? How will you be different if you *don't* develop as a Christian? Take a few moments to picture yourself as you can be, and ask God to fulfill that vision according to His will.

- Read Colossians 3:16. Where will you find "the teaching of Christ"? How is it possible for it to "live in you richly"?

- Read 1 Timothy 4:13. Why did Paul tell this to Timothy? Was the reading of the Scriptures important to Paul? to Timothy? to you?

- Read 2 Timothy 3:15–17. Notice the many things these short verses say about the Bible:

they are "the ___*holy*___ Scriptures" (v. 15)

they are able to ___*make you wise*___ (v. 15).

the wisdom they give leads to ___*salvation*___ (v. 15)

they are given to us by ___*God*___ (v. 16)

they are useful for ___*to teach us what*___
___*is true & make us realize what*___
___*is wrong in our lives*___ (v. 16)

the person who uses them will be ___*well prepared*___
___*fully equipped to do good*___ (v. 17)

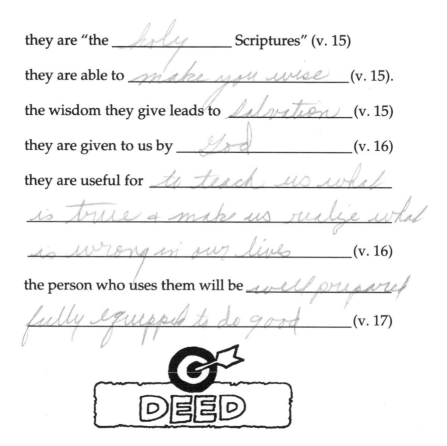

- One reason many young Christians find Bible study so difficult is that no one has really given them simple guidelines for personal study, such as the following:

  Spend 15–30 minutes a day in Bible study. As you sit down to read, ask the Holy Spirit to help you understand what you study.

Use a Bible translation you can understand. Start by studying the book of Mark, John, or Romans.

Keep a notebook and pencil close by for jotting notes. For each section you read, ask yourself: What is the main point of this section? What does it teach me about God, Jesus Christ, and the Holy Spirit? What does it teach me about myself? What am I going to do about what I learned?

Conclude by thanking God for what you learned. Ask Him for the confidence and power you need to apply His Word to your life.

- Day 2   Read Romans 1:16–17. Praise God today for the gift of His Word; also ask Him to increase your interest in it and enjoyment of it.

- Day 3   Read Romans 15:1–4. Open your prayer time:

   Father, I praise You for the patience and encouragement that the Scriptures give me. Please help me to receive Your Word gladly today. Amen.

   Follow this by presenting your requests to God.

- Day 4   Read Hebrews 4:12–13, substituting the words, "me," "my," and "I" for "us," "our," and "we." Conclude with prayers of praise and petition.

- Day 5   Read 1 Peter 1:22–2:2. Spend time in praise, confession, and thanksgiving; then present your requests to God.

- Day 6   Read 2 Peter 1:16–21. Conclude your time of Bible reading and prayer with these words:

> *Father, the message of Your Word is like a light shining in a dark place. Make it shine until the day begins and the Morning Star—the Lord Jesus—rises in my heart. Amen.*

•   Day 7   Read Revelation 1:1–3. Are you finding enjoyment and success in reading God's Word? If so, thank Him. If not, continue to seek the answer to your prayer: strength from the Word.

Together you are the body of Christ, and each one of you is a part of that body.

1 Corinthians 12:27

10

Duane's Support

"I got a little cocky, I guess," Duane Cunningham admitted to Marlon Trask.

Duane had picked Marlon up on the way home from work and treated him to a Tornado Shake at the Icee Freeze. He still wore the dirty-jeans-and-t-shirt uniform of the construction site.

Duane had expressed some concern for Marlon. He pointed out that though Marlon had attended church with Will and Dorinna McConnell the first few months after he prayed for salvation, he hadn't seen him in church lately.

Marlon had answered that he'd decided to attend his uncle's church and try to encourage the youth group to begin rescue efforts like the Liberation Commandos.

After dipping another spoonful of the ice cream mixture, Duane had responded, "That sounds like a really great idea, Marlon." He then went on to explain, as he had planned, the reason he thought church attendance was so important.

He told Marlon about those exciting college days when he'd led a campus prayer group that had brought several people to faith in Christ, and how that group had become so important and rewarding to him. Sometimes the victories and growth he experienced because of the campus group made the church he was attending seem a little dull by comparison, so he began to think he didn't need the church.

"I really thought, at the time, that I could be that rare creature I'd heard about once in a while but never actually

saw—a Lone-Ranger Christian, a Christian who could live and grow without a church fellowship.

"I realize now how arrogant that was. But back then it seemed like, well, I had my Bible, I knew how to pray pretty much, and I really didn't need anything else."

Marlon surprised himself with a loud slurp from his straw. He cowered and looked around, embarrassed. Duane blushed with embarrassment, too—at the remembrance of his experience as he talked.

It had been only five or six years.

◆ ◆ ◆

At first, Duane rationalized that sleeping in on Sundays was making him more effective in his studies and that not going to church cleared more time for personal prayer and Bible study.

But over the course of several weeks, he began to be aware of a deterioration in his Christian life: his praying seemed flat, the Bible lost much of its color, and he felt—for the first time since becoming a Christian—alone.

It makes no sense, he reasoned. *Nothing has changed. It shouldn't affect me as it has. My personal praying and Bible study have nothing to do with going to church. My life as a Christian is between me and the Lord, not a couple hundred other people. Besides, I have all kinds of friends right here, in the campus prayer group—why should I feel lonely and isolated?*

Still, for all his reasoning, he couldn't reverse the decline in his spiritual life.

Finally, one Saturday evening, Duane decided to return to church. *I'll just slip in quietly, and act as though I'd never stopped. I'll sit somewhere near the back,* he concluded.

He couldn't do it.

When he slapped off the alarm on Sunday morning, he immediately remembered his resolution to go to church that day. He ignored it and went back to sleep.

Late Sunday night, he scolded himself and determined to return to his church the following week.

He failed again.

This is ridiculous, he told himself. *I've been going to that church since the first or second week of my freshman year—why is it so hard all of a sudden?*

He realized, then, that it hadn't happened "all of a sudden." Every week that he'd neglected Sunday worship, he had just made it harder for himself to return.

"*Next* Sunday," he said. "Next Sunday morning I am going."

Saturday night, he laid his clothes out on his chair and placed his Bible neatly beside them.

When his alarm sounded Sunday morning, he smacked it without opening his eyes. His mind registered: *Sunday*. He opened one eye, peered at the digital clock face of the alarm clock, and closed it again.

When next he opened his eyes, the message on the clock prompted him to sit up on the side of the bed, throwing the covers off vigorously at the same time.

I'm late. I'll never make it.

He showered, dressed, and hopped out the front door of his dorm still pulling a shoe on and trying to tie it with his Bible in one hand. He lost his balance, breaking his fall with the heels of his hands, losing his Bible, and trying to keep his knees from contacting the cement sidewalk.

Duane uprighted himself and inspected his knees: no damage. He sighed with relief. Then he was aware of a burning in his palms. He turned his hands over. They were an ugly mixture of blood red and dirt black. He considered turning back into the dorm, but clenched his jaw with determination. *I'll wash as soon as I get in the front door.*

He walked the short distance to the church. The morning worship service had begun. Avoiding the gaze of the ushers at the sanctuary doors, he bent his head toward the washroom, slipped in, washed his hands gingerly, combed his hair, and stepped back into the foyer. The ushers had closed the doors and entered the sanctuary.

A voice inside his head suggested, *This isn't the week. Wait until next week; you can get here on time then.*

He hesitated only briefly before heading for the wide doors he had entered moments ago and descended the stone steps of the church. He walked briskly to the corner and stopped to wait for the "Walk" light.

Next week, the voice repeated. *Next week would be better.*

The light changed. He didn't move.

Next week, it came again. He shifted his feet nervously.

"I've come this far," he said out loud. A woman led by a chihuahua on a leash stepped to the curb beside him. She looked at the "Walk" signal, which had just begun flashing. She looked at Duane, then back at the signal. "Don't Walk" appeared.

"I've come this far," he repeated. The woman and chihuahua turned their heads together to look at him again, but he had wheeled around.

As he grasped the handle of the church door, he whispered a prayer.

"Lord, I'm sorry. Meet me here. Please."

◆ ◆ ◆

"So I just wanted to make sure that you don't make the mistake I made," Duane told Marlon. "Being part of a church fellowship is crucial to the Christian.

"It's not only participating in worship or learning from Bible study; it's also being responsible to other Christians, feeling their support, being inspired by their example, and learning from their failures.

"And, I guess most importantly, it's one of those things the Bible commands. So in addition to being foolish when I thought I could live the Christian life without the support of the church, I was also being disobedient."

Duane and Marlon rose from the table, gathered their cups and spoons and straws and stuffed them into the waste can as they left the Icee Freeze.

PowerLink   PowerThink

"I can worship God just as well in the forest or in a garden as I can in a church." Have you ever heard anyone express an idea like that?

It's a fairly common opinion.

The problem is—it's not true. From the beginning of time, God has had a plan to bring people to salvation and on to Christian maturity—and that plan has involved the Church. God intends for the followers of Jesus Christ to gather together to worship Him and fellowship together. That's why His word commands, "You should not stay away from the church meetings, as some are doing. But you should meet together and encourage each other. Do this even more as you see the Day[5] approaching."

- Why do you think it became increasingly harder for Duane to return to his church the longer he stayed away?

- What do you think about Duane's reasoning: *It shouldn't affect me as it has. My personal praying and Bible study have nothing to do with going to church. My life as a Christian is between me and the Lord, not a couple hundred other people. Besides, I have all kinds of friends right here, in the campus prayer group—why should I feel lonely and isolated?* How do you react to that? What would you say to Duane?

---

5. The day of Christ's return

- God's Word describes the Church in a variety of ways, using a variety of images. Read the Scripture passages below, and in the blanks provided, identify what the Bible compares the Church to:

  1 Corinthians 3:9 _____

  1 Corinthians 12:27 _____

  Luke 12:32 _____

  Revelation 21:2 _____

- Now take a few moments to think about those images; in what way are they like the Church? How do those attributes fulfill a Christian's needs?

- Do you have a church fellowship of your own? If not, ask God to lead you to a church in which you can worship, fellowship, learn, and serve. Be patient in allowing God to show you His choice, but make sure that you are in the Lord's House every Lord's Day.

- If you have a church home, spend a few moments in prayer, thanking God for your church, asking Him to teach you and nurture you through it, offering yourself as His servant in that fellowship.

- Express a personal interest in one person in your church fellowship (outside your current circle of friends) by making special note of his or her presence or absence. When he is present, make an extra effort to say "hello" or "good to see you." When he is absent, go out of your way to let him know he was missed.

- Day 2   Read Ephesians 2:19–22. After prayers of praise and thanks to God, pray:

  Father, thank You that I am not a visitor or a stranger to the Church, but a citizen together with God's people. I belong to Your family! Thank You. Amen.

- Day 3   Read Ephesians 5:8–14. Close with prayer for that person you've chosen to express a personal interest in.

- Day 4   Read Colossians 1:15–22. Praise God for the Church, for *your* church, and for your pastor(s). Close with prayer for that person you've chosen to express a personal interest in.

- Day 5   Read 1 Timothy 3:14–16. Pray for the needs of your church. Close with prayer for that person you've chosen to express a personal interest in.

- Day 6   Read Hebrews 2:10–13. Now *pray* those verses in praise to God (for example, "*You* are the One who made all things. . . ").

- Day 7   Read Hebrews 12:18–24. After your prayer time, close with:

  Father, thank You for bringing me to the city of the Living God, to the fellowship of the Church. As I grow as a Christian, help me never to forget the importance of the meeting of God's firstborn children. Amen.

All those who stand before others and say they believe in me, I will say before my Father in heaven that they belong to me.

Matthew 10:32

11

Buster's Passion

The quarterback crumpled beneath the linebacker's crushing weight.

Buster Todd, watching from the stands, jumped to his feet. He held his breath while the linebacker who had sacked his best friend John pumped a fist in the air.

"Got him from his blind side," Buster's dad said, feeling his son's tense concern. Buster, Mr. Todd, and the rest of the crowd waited for some signal from the coaches and players leaning over the Dover High quarterback to indicate whether he was seriously hurt.

A wave of applause swept the crowd when the huddle parted and John Dexter, Number 7, emerged. He walked slowly—but without help—to the sidelines.

"I was out cold for a few seconds, I guess," John told Buster later that night at McDonald's. "I wanted to get back in the game, but Coach thought I should sit it out just in case. Shane played a good quarter, didn't he?"

"He did o-o-okay," Buster stammered out. He knew what John wanted to hear. "But he'll n-n-never take your place."

The two had been close friends for several years. They called themselves "The Odd Couple" privately, because it would be difficult to find two more different "best friends." John started as quarterback for Dover High in his freshman year; Buster, who considered himself hopelessly unathletic, preferred to spend hours working on his dad's car. John's good looks and personality made him popular with guys and girls; Buster withdrew at times because of his slight speech impediment. John's parents considered religion a crutch for the weak; Buster's parents were devoted Christians.

"So," Buster said, after assuring John that he was a better quarterback than Shane Mitchell, a sophomore, who was unhappy at starting his second year now as second-string quarterback. "Wh-, whatcha doing Sunday?"

John shrugged his shoulders as he sipped his chocolate shake. "Dad talked about going to the Pumpkin Festival in Nelson." He sipped again. "He'll probably work, though."

Buster nodded. He played with the straw in his empty cup. He had intended to invite John to church, and maybe talk to him about Christ. He'd made several feeble attempts to tell his best friend about what it means to be a Christian, but he could never seem to get anywhere. He wished John were a Christian. He imagined how great it would be to go to Sunday school and church with John. He knew the command of Jesus, to "go and make followers of all people in the world." But deep in his heart, he admitted that he was worried John might be angry or irritated if Buster were to witness to him, and he didn't want to damage their friendship.

They left the restaurant and grabbed their ten-speeds.

"Hey," John said. "When Dad gets me my car, we can put these bikes away for good."

"Yeah. And I-uh-I'll keep it running for you. I-I'll call you tomorrow."

"Later." John straddled his bike and turned down the dark street behind the restaurant, while Buster pedalled the opposite way toward home.

Buster heard the phone down the hall. He pried one eye open and gazed at the digital numbers: 2:00 A.M. He listened for a moment, closed his eye and was asleep instantly.

Moments later, his mother's arm on his shoulder woke him. She sat on the edge of his bed, whispering his name.

"Mrs. Dexter's on the phone," she explained when he sat up. "It's important."

Buster picked up the phone.

"This is John's mother. I hoped he'd be with you."

Buster stuttered a few disjointed syllables into the phone.

"John hasn't come home yet," Mrs. Dexter explained, her voice trembling now. "He never came home after the football game. Do you—do you know where he is?"

Buster froze. He struggled to make words come out of his mouth. "No," he said finally. "I- I- I- " He stopped, then started again. "W-w-we left McDonald's before midnight. He was going ho-ome."

"He—" Mrs. Dexter blurted the word out before her voice was choked by sobs. Buster listened helplessly, silently.

"Buster?" A man's voice sounded in Buster's ear. "Buster? This is Jim Dexter, John's dad. If you hear from him, will you call us—immediately?"

"Y-y-yessir, I will," Buster answered. The call ended abruptly with a "thank you" and a click.

Buster repeated the conversation to his mother, who disappeared into her bedroom while he began dressing.

The next forty-eight hours were a sleepless blur of police, neighbors, friends, and reporters. A systematic search for John was conducted, posters appeared immediately on poles and bulletin boards, and his description was repeated on television and radio news.

God, please let him be okay, Buster prayed. *Please don't let anything happen to him.* He prayed not only for John's benefit, but for himself, too: he feared that he'd missed his last opportunity to tell his best friend about salvation in Christ. *I could never live with the thought of John in hell,* he thought.

Buster continued to search, pray, and phone long after many others had given up. He occasionally tried to convince himself that John had gotten lost, or forgotten his house key and stayed at a friend's house, or other unlikely explanations. He imagined heroically finding John pinned beneath a fallen tree and joyously reuniting him with his parents. For most of two weeks, Buster Todd slept little and cried much.

When Buster's father, a Captain in the U.S. Army, informed the family that they would have to move to a new home several states away, John's disappearance remained a mystery—a mystery that had traumatized Buster for months.

Except for a tearful farewell to Mr. and Mrs. Dexter, Buster plodded through the process of moving to Westcastle, enrolling in a new school, and joining a new church like a sleepy creature in a bad monster movie.

Buster began the year at Eisenhower High in Westcastle as a painfully quiet, lonely sophomore—until he met Bill Engel in shop class. The two hit it off immediately. They shared many common interests and abilities, like a talent for building and rebuilding nearly anything mechanical.

Buster was thrilled to find out that Bill's family attended church. "What church?" he asked.

"Well," Bill shrugged. "It's no big deal. I don't really like it. I think we just go because Mom thinks we should, because her parents made her go when she was a kid."

Buster frowned. "You- you're not a Christian, then?"

Bill turned both palms up. "Well yeah, sure I'm a Christian, didn't I just tell you?"

Buster felt a strong urge to back off and end the conversation with a shrug and a change in subject. His stomach knotted. *He's your first friend here,* he told himself. *Don't blow it so soon.* But he remembered the many struggles, promises, and resolutions of the past several months. *Yeah. That's exactly right. Don't blow it so soon.*

"No. You- you told me you go to church. I-it's not the same thing." Bill looked at Buster with surprise. "You- you want me to tell you what it means to be a Christian?"

Bill said nothing, but nodded his head slightly. Buster blushed with embarrassment and fear, but began to explain— with many stops and stutters—the simple steps to salvation in Christ.

Ten minutes later, when Buster bowed his head to pray with Bill, a quiet voice seemed to whisper a promise to his heart.

This is just the beginning, Buster, it seemed to say.

PowerLink   PowerThink

Many people, when they first experience the forgiveness of sins and freedom from guilt that salvation in Christ brings, feel a compelling urge to tell somebody—perhaps everybody. Others, however, treat their salvation like it's a secret.

It's important, early in your new life in Christ, to begin to obey Jesus' command to "go and make followers of all people in the world." This next "PowerLink/PowerThink" section can help equip you to introduce your friends to the Best Friend they can possibly know.

- Do you find it difficult to tell people about your experience of salvation?

- Do you find it easier to tell friends, family, or strangers about Christ?

- What scares you the most about talking to others about Christ?

- What is the worst you suppose could happen if you witness openly to others? The best?

- What is the worst you suppose could happen if you *don't* witness openly to others? The best?

- Read the following examples of successful "witnesses" of Jesus. Consider as you read: What made them speak? What did they say? What were the keys to their success?

  John 1:41–42
  John 1:45
  John 4:3–15, 27–30
  1 Corinthians 9:20

- Make a list of those among your friends and family you'd like to see come to Christ (like Will McConnell's list in *Under Siege*).

- Pray for the people on that list every day, asking God for the opportunity to tell them about your experience of salvation.

- Begin actively looking for opportunities, for openings in conversations, such as Buster found in his conversation with Bill.

- Learn from your failures. When you miss a chance or fail to make the best of an opportunity to tell a friend about Christ, learn something from it that will help you to succeed the next time.

- Keep at it. Don't give up.

- Add new names to your list as God answers your prayers and increases your effectiveness in introducing your friends to Jesus Christ.

- Day 2   Read Matthew 10:32 and Luke 12:8. After prayers of praise and thanks to God, pray:

  Father, help me to stand up before others and say that I believe in and follow You. Help me to share my experience of new life through Jesus Christ. Amen.

- Day 3   Read Acts 5:17–24. Pray for those on your "most wanted list," then:

  Father, again I ask You to help me "tell the people everything about this new life." Amen.

- Day 4   Read Acts 5:25–32. Pray for those on your list, ending with prayer for courage and effectiveness in witnessing.

- Day 5   Read 2 Timothy 1:3–8. Close your prayer time with the following:

  Father, I thank You that You did not give me a spirit that makes me afraid, but a spirit of power and love and self-control. So help me not to be ashamed to tell people about my Lord Jesus. Amen.

- Day 6   Read James 5:19–20. Thank God for the person God used to tell you about salvation in Christ.

- Day 7   Read 1 Peter 3:10–15. After your prayer time, close with:

  Father, I have many fears. I commit them to You and ask You to help me to fear only the tragedy that awaits those who do not accept your offer of eternal life. In Jesus' name, Amen.

My dear children, I write this letter to you so you will not sin. But if anyone does sin, we have a helper in the presence of the Father—Jesus Christ, the One who does what is right.

1 John 2:1

12

Tony's Mistake

Tony pummelled the door with his fist.

The door swung open. Will McConnell opened his mouth, but Tony shouldered past him without a word and bounded the steps to Will's room.

Tony sat heavily on Will's bed. Seconds later, Will entered breathlessly. The two stared at each other.

Tony broke the silence.

"Will," he said, "I don't know if I can explain what happened to me. It was that booklet—the prayer in that booklet—I couldn't get it out of my mind."

Tony had shown up at Will's house following a disastrous pizza party several days ago. Will and Marlon had shared a brief testimony with him and Will had read through the booklet *Would You Like to Know God Personally?* with Tony. When Will had asked him if he was ready to trust Christ, Tony had panicked and raced out of the room. Now, four days later, he had just as rashly returned.

Will leaned forward in anticipation as Tony continued.

"When I left your place I just kept driving. I went all the way to my cousin's place upstate. And on the way I kept praying that prayer from the booklet. I think I did it!"

Will read his indecision clearly. "Well, Tony, did you really mean it when you prayed, opening your life to Christ and trusting Him as your Savior?"

Tony paused. "Yeah, I really did."

Will's heart pounded with excitement. After a few seconds of frantic thought and prayer, he asked, "Then where is Christ today, right now?"

Again Tony paused to weigh his feelings against the facts. "I guess He's in my life."

Will went on without hesitation. "Remember Revelation 3:20?" He tapped the reference into his computer's Bible concordance. The verse flashed up on the monitor. "Read this part again."

Tony scooted closer to the screen. "If anyone hears my voice and opens the door, I will come in."

"Did you open the door?" Will pressed.

"Yeah."

"Did Christ come in?"

"Yeah."

"Then, according to this verse, where is He right now?"

Tony smiled and tapped his chest with his finger. "Right here."

"That's right, Tony. He's there because you trusted Him to forgive your sins and invited Him to come in—and He did. The devil will try to convince you that you're no different because you don't feel any different. Feelings come and go, but Jesus doesn't. He's there to stay."

That evening at Will's house had confirmed Tony's experience of salvation. Even after his first full week as a newborn Christian, the football star felt completely new and different.

"It's a rush, man," he explained to Hooper, one of his friends from the football team. They sat in Hooper's room, surrounded by posters of girls in swimsuits and athletes in uniform. "It's nothing like those guys on TV make it sound. It's real."

Hooper nodded uncomfortably. "Thirsty?" he asked. Tony shrugged and Hooper disappeared for a few minutes while Tony returned to flipping through the latest issue of *Sports Illustrated.*

Hooper slipped through the door and swung it shut behind him. "Almost got caught," he whispered. Tony looked up just as Hooper tossed him a beer can. After a moment of indecision, Tony pried the can open, raised it in a toast, and gulped heartily.

Later, stimulated by a couple more beers, the two friends jumped into Tony's car. Tony screeched out of Hooper's driveway without a plan; minutes later, however, he skidded to a stop in the gravel drive of The Cave.

"Hey, wait a minute, Tony. Isn't this Craig's night off?"

Tony halted and whispered, "I never get carded here—Craig or no Craig."

The two high school seniors entered the bar. A live band shook the walls with pounding rhythms. Tony and Hooper strolled into the smoky dimness of the room, slowly turning their heads from side to side, looking for empty tables and lone females.

Tony jabbed Hooper in the ribs. "There." He strutted to a corner table and sat beside a pretty girl with short blonde hair. Hooper took another empty chair and listened to Tony's smooth patter with admiration.

Tony held the girl's chair as she stood. He felt a hand on his shoulder. He turned and saw Duane Cunningham, the youth group leader from Westcastle Community Church.

"Duane. What's up?"

"What's up?" Duane echoed. "You have to ask?" He turned to the girl. "Would you excuse us?"

She looked from Duane to Tony.

"Uh," Tony started awkwardly. "This was her table." He slid out from behind the table and began walking to the door. Duane followed.

As soon as they cleared the door, Duane gripped Tony's arm and pulled him to the corner of the building.

"What?" Tony asked, brushing Duane's hand away as if it were a pesky fly.

"What is wrong with you, Tony? Doesn't your relationship with Christ mean anything to you?"

"What the—what are you talking about?"

"Didn't we just go through this the other night? You're a Christian, Tony. What's a follower of Christ doing here picking up a girl?" He stopped and inhaled sharply. "With beer on his breath?" he added emphatically.

Tony crossed his arms and pursed his lips. The two glared at each other in silence.

"Okay," Tony finally said. "I'm sorry."

"You're sorry?" Duane asked. "You're sorry?"

"Yeah, I'm sorry, okay?"

"Tony, you were sorry two or three days ago when I confronted you about your behavior. You were sorry the day before that. When are you going to stop being sorry and start being obedient?"

Tony shifted his weight. He tightened his crossed arms on his chest.

"Christ saved you, didn't He? You trusted in His blood as payment for your sins, didn't you? He entered your life, right?"

"Yeah. It's just going to take time, okay? Look, I'll confess everything when I get home."

Duane stared at Tony. Finally, he said, "It's not a big deal to you, is it? You just disobey now and confess it later, right?"

Tony dropped his gaze and stared at the ground. When he looked at Duane again, he did it without lifting his head. "Look. I know I'm new at this, but I thought that was kind of the idea— that God's supposed to forgive me because of Jesus."

Duane began to speak, but stopped. He looked around him in the dark parking lot. "Where's your car?" he asked. Before Tony could answer, he said, "Never mind. Let's go sit in the truck."

Duane leaned over in the cab of the pickup and pulled a New Testament out of the glove compartment. He switched on the cab light and fingered through the thin pages. Finally, he stopped, closed a fingertip in the testament, and looked Tony squarely in the eyes.

"I hope you're completely sincere and not trying to pull the wool over my eyes, Tony, because this is really important stuff." He opened to the place he had held and extended the New Testament in Tony's direction. "I want you to read. Here," he said, pointing to the page. "First John, chapter two."

Tony studied the page, his eyes moving from side to side.

"No, I mean out loud," Duane added.

"Oh." Tony found the point where he had begun. "My dear children, I write this letter to you so you will not sin. But if anyone does sin, we have a helper in the presence of the Father—Jesus Christ, the One who does what is right. He is the way our sins are taken away, and not only our sins but the sins of all people. We can be sure that we know God if we obey his commands."

"Stop," Duane said. "Catch that?"

Tony reread the verses silently.

"John says, 'I write this letter so you will not sin.' Right? *If* you sin, he says, we have a helper in Christ, and we can be forgiven. But don't miss the last part I had you read. What did it say—" Duane leaned over the page. "Read verse 3 again."

"We can be sure that we know God if we obey his commands."

Duane closed the New Testament. "Don't make the mistake of thinking that because God's forgiveness is free, it's cheap. Because it's not. Jesus endured the agony of the cross not only so you could be forgiven, but also so you could be obedient."

Tony said nothing, but the sober, intense gleam in his eyes indicated that he understood. For a few moments, the two stared at each other, conscious of a radiance that seemed to fill the truck, even in that darkness. Tony's jaw tightened."I think I want to pray," he said.

"You first," Duane said.

PowerLink   PowerThink

Young Christians occasionally overlook the importance of obedience. If you know God will forgive you, why not do what you want and ask Him for forgiveness later? Because God forgives the repentant heart; and repentance means being sorry for your sin—sorry enough to change your mind about sin.

Concentrate your thought, word, and deed on avoiding Tony's mistake.

- Think about Duane's statement to Tony, "Don't make the mistake of thinking that because God's forgiveness is free, it's cheap. Because it's not." What is the difference between something that's *free* and something that's *cheap?*

- How do you know God's forgiveness is not cheap? What did it cost?

- Turn to the Gospel of John, chapter 14. Read John 14:15 through John 15:11. Then look back to the following verses and, in the spaces provided, put the "If . . .then" statement of that verse into your own words.

        John 14:15   If _____

                     then _____.

        John 14:23   If _____

                     then _____.

        John 15:5   If _____

                     then _____.

John 15:10   If _____

then _____ .

DEED

• A helpful practice to begin is to conclude each week or each month with a personal inventory. Ask yourself such questions as:

Have I been obedient in my relationship with my Lord? Have I been faithful to Him in prayer and Bible study?

Have I been obedient in my relationships with others? Have my temper and my tongue been under control? Have I been kind? patient? thoughtful? caring?

Has my thought life been under the Spirit's control? Have I resisted temptations to lust? envy? greed? hatred? worry? pride?

Have I been slow to respond to the Lord's prodding, leading me in a new direction or down a new path of obedience? Or am I following the light He gives me, step by step?

Am I being obedient in my responsibilities at school? at home? church?

What sins or temptations plague me most? Am I on guard against them?

What new way can I submit to God's will for me? What new area of my life can I surrender to His control?

You may wish to add to or subtract from this inventory until you find a series of questions that will help you "look closely at yourselves. Test yourselves to see if you are living in the faith" (1 Corinthians 13:5).

- Day 2   Read Hebrews 2:1–3. After prayers of praise and petition, close with:

   Father, thank You for the great salvation You've given to me. I want to be careful to follow what I've been taught, so that I will not be pulled away from the truth. Please, never let me live as if my salvation were not important. Amen.

- Day 3   Read Hebrews 5:7–9. Reflect on the several ways mentioned in these verses that Christ has given you an example to follow. Close in prayer.

- Day 4   Read James 1:22–25. After your time of praise and petition, pray a prayer based on these verses (for example, "Lord, help me to do what Your teaching says . . .").

- Day 5   Read 1 John 2:1–6. Close your prayer time with the following:

   Father, I bless You and thank You for Jesus, the Righteous One, who defends me when I sin. Create in me a clean heart, and one that is obedient to You. Amen.

- Day 6   Read 1 John 3:21–24. After presenting your praise and petitions to God, spend some time listening to Him, asking Him to reveal ways in which you can be more obedient to Him.

- Day 7   Read 1 John 5:1–5. After your prayer time, close with this prayer or a similar one of your own:

Father, I know that loving You means obeying Your commands. And I know, too, that Your commands are not too hard for me. I thank You that I have the power to win against the world. Help me to trust You for that victory as I seek to obey You more and more. Amen.

So those who suffer as God wants should trust their souls to the faithful Creator as they continue to do what is right.

1 Peter 4:19

13

Hillary's Key

"Stop fighting!"

Hillary Putnam snatched seven-year-old Andrea by the shoulders and sat her on the side of the swimming pool. The little girl snorted and sniffed, sobbed and shivered before her swim instructor.

"Andy," Hillary said, trying to restrain her frustration, "you've absolutely *got* to stop fighting the water."

"But, but, but I was going under," the redhead squeaked, then broke into sobs again.

"Like I was going to let anything happen to you. I'm sure. You've *got* to stop—oh, never mind." She glanced at the clock on the wall between the shower rooms. "It's almost time, anyway. Go get your shower."

Hillary whistled the other students out of the pool and subconsciously shook her head. *She's the worst,* she thought. *I've never had anybody so afraid to relax in the water. I honestly don't know what I'm going to do with her.*

Hillary stopped by Amber Lockwood's house after swim class. The two had grown close since Christmas. Amber had shared the gospel with Hillary during a shopping trip and Hillary had prayed to trust Christ right there in front of the Penney's store at Westcastle Mall.

"She's in her room," Amber's mother said as soon as she opened the door to Hillary.

Hillary peeked into her friend's room. Amber looked up;

she sat cross-legged on her bed, a Bible on her lap. Hillary sat down facing Amber, crossing her legs.

"How's it going?" Amber asked.

Hillary shrugged. The smile and bright eyes with which she'd greeted Amber faded now.

"What's wrong?"

Hillary shrugged again. "I don't know."

"Same thing, huh?"

Hillary said nothing, but clicked her fingernails together.

"Hillary, this isn't like you at all. You're usually the one to cheer *me* up."

"You keep saying that I need to stop trying so much and just trust. Well, I can't. I mean, you have to try. You have to do this and not do that, right?"

Amber blinked at Hillary, surprised at the sudden shift in the conversation. She uncrossed her legs, curled one underneath herself and hung the other over the edge of the bed.

"I just don't get it," Hillary continued. "If I, like, steal something, I'm sinning. So I should try not to steal. But you say I shouldn't try so much, I should just trust. And I don't know what you mean."

Amber inhaled deeply, thinking. "It's . . ." she started, paused, then began again. "Of course you should try not to steal. But if stealing is a big temptation to you, then *trying* won't keep you from stealing—only trusting Christ will do it."

"I don't see," Hillary said, "I don't see how that works. I don't get the difference." She stood. Amber had opened her mouth to speak, but closed it again when Hillary stood. "I have to do some things with my mom this afternoon. I'll talk to you later."

Amber smiled weakly as Hillary left.

Throughout the afternoon, as Hillary waited for her mom at the beauty parlor, she recalled her many conversations with Amber and with Liz Cunningham.

"You can struggle all you want," Liz had said, "to overcome temptation. And it may work sometimes. But gritting your teeth and resisting only goes so far. That's why the Israelites—in the Old Testament days—kept falling into sin, because sooner or later the temptation will overcome you. But the reason Christ died and ascended and lives in you now is so that He can *give* you victory—if you trust in Him."

Still, it seemed to Hillary that the harder she tried, the weaker she became; the more she pressed, the more she failed. Every day, she determined anew to win the battle against temptation; every night her discouragement grew. She flipped through a magazine in the beauty parlor waiting area and recalled another talk with Liz.

"It's like that old hymn, *Trust and Obey*. It goes, 'Trust and obey, for there's no other way to be happy in Jesus, but to *trust and obey*.' Those are the two ingredients for victory in the Christian life. You have no problem with the obey part—you understand that. But the trust part is the one you can't quite grasp, right?"

"Right," Hillary said. She realized suddenly that the ladies in the little waiting area were staring at her. She had blurted the word out loud, forgetting where she was and answering Liz's question as if it were taking place in the present. She blinked at the staring women. "Good article," she said, lifting the magazine and smiling sheepishly.

Westcastle Mall teemed with Saturday shoppers. Hillary elbowed through the crowds with her mother.

"Hillary!" A voice squealed her name somewhere in the press of bodies and shopping bags. Hillary spun her head around.

"Hillary!" The voice called again.

"Oh hi, Andy." Hillary spied the redheaded girl from her swim class standing at her left elbow. "Are you here by yourself?"

"No, Mommy's over there." Andrea pointed to a woman in a flowered dress, sitting in front of a fountain, surrounded by large bags from every major store in the mall.

Hillary was reminded of her own mother, who had stopped several feet in front of where she and Andrea stood.

"Oh," Hillary said. "Mom, this is Andrea." She looked at Andrea. "This is my mom, Mrs. Putnam."

"This is the girl I told you about, Mom." Hillary fastened

her sparkling eyes on Andrea. "I'll bet she could swim in the
Olympics if she could just stop *fighting* the water." The redhead
blushed, but smiled affectionately back at Hillary.

"She can float like a—well, I don't know what—but when
she tries to swim, she forgets that she doesn't have to do all the
work. The water will do most of the work if she just lets it. Isn't
that right, Andy?"

"Right." Andrea barked the word as though everything
Hillary said had been her idea.

Hillary froze for a moment, remembering the scene in the
beauty parlor, when she had said the same word, out loud, with
the same conviction Andrea had just voiced.

"Next week, Andrea, I'm going to teach you how to trust,
okay?"

"Okay. Bye, Hillary!"

Can it really be that simple? Hillary wondered as she and her
mother resumed their winding walk through the mall. *I've been
so frustrated with Andy because she won't believe the water can
support her weight. She thinks she has to do all the work. But all she
has to do is to trust the water's ability to hold her—and—*she shifted
her thought—*all I have to do is trust the Lord's ability to hold me. Like
Liz said, "The reason Christ died and ascended and lives in you now
is so that He can* give *you victory—if you trust in Him."*

"Go on ahead, Mom," Hillary said. "I think I just want to
sit here for a few minutes." She sat on a bench opposite the
Penney's store entrance and smiled at the remembrance of what
had taken place in this very spot several months ago.

She began praying, out loud but in a low voice, "Lord, this
is where I first trusted You to forgive my sins. I trust You still—
to give me victory over temptation and sin. Help me to really
learn how to throw my whole weight on Your ability to hold me.
And if You'll teach me to trust You every day—every minute—
for victory, I'll move my arms and kick my legs and add my
effort to Your support. But I'll realize that You're the One doing
the work. Amen."

A few moments later, Hillary joined her mom in the store,
whistling the tune *Trust and Obey*.

PowerLink   PowerThink

Hillary's difficulty understanding the importance of trusting in Christ rather than a teeth-gritting effort against temptation is a crucial lesson for a new Christian—and for some old ones, too! Willpower won't save you from sin; only Jesus can do that.

Use the following "PowerLink/PowerThink" to help solidify this concept in your mind and heart.

- Can you swim? If so, try to recall how you learned. Did you learn quickly? Was it hard or easy? Did you have Andrea's problem of "fighting" the water?

- If you can't swim, why haven't you learned? What prevents you? Fear? Lack of a teacher? Something else?

- Review your answers to the above questions. Do any of them apply to the lesson of this chapter?

- Read Matthew 27:41–43, a description of events during the crucifixion of Jesus. What do you think the mockers meant, "He trusts in God?"

- Read Romans 4:4–5. Some of the most important words in these verses are the "connecting" words: but, so, then, and. Underline each of those words and then re-read these verses, placing particular emphasis on those words.

- Read Romans 9:31–33 and 1 Peter 2:4–6. What do these two references have in common? Notice that in Romans 9:31–33, Paul uses the same illustration as Liz in the chapter above. If we do not "follow a law to make [ourselves] right with God," how do we do it?

- Look back to Hillary's prayer in the mall. If possible, sometime this week, go to the place where you first prayed for salvation in Christ, and pray Hillary's prayer. As you read it aloud, be careful to truly pray it, concentrating not only on the words but on the intentions and determination it expresses.

- Day 2   Read Ephesians 4:1–10. After prayers of praise to God, pray a prayer based on verses 7–10. For example, "Jesus, I thank You that You gave each one of us a special gift. Thank You that I received what You wanted to give me" (v. 7). Close with prayers of petition.

- Day 3   Read Colossians 2:6–10. Reflect on the meaning of verse 6: How did you receive Christ? How should you continue to live in Him? Close in prayer.

- Day 4   Read 1 Peter 2:19–25. Close your prayer time with a request for God's help in teaching you to trust.

- Day 5   Read 1 Peter 4:12–19. Close your prayer time
            with the following, based on verse 19:

      Father, I trust my soul to You. You are the One who
      made me, and I know I can trust You. Help me to
      continue to do what is right. Amen.

- Day 6   Read 1 John 2:1–6. After presenting your praise
            and petitions to God, pray a prayer of thanks to
            Him, based on these verses.

- Day 7   Read 1 John 5:18–20. After your prayer time,
            repeat Hillary's prayer of trust from the chapter
            above, making it truly your own prayer once
            more.

If you have grown personally as a result of this material, we should stay in touch. You will want to continue in your Christian growth, and to help your faith become even stronger, our team is constantly developing new materials.

We publish a monthly newsletter called **5 Minutes with Josh** which will:

1) tell you about those new materials as they become available,
2) answer your tough questions,
3) give creative tips on being an effective parent,
4) let you know our ministry needs, and
5) keep you up-to-date on my speaking schedule (so you can pray).

If you would like to receive this publication, simply fill out the coupon below and send it in. By special arrangement **5 Minutes with Josh** will come to you regularly — <u>no charge</u>.

Let's keep in touch!

Josh

Yes! I want to receive the free subscription to **5 Minutes with JOSH**

Name_____

Address_____

City_____State_____Zip_____

Mail to: Josh McDowell Ministry, **5 Minutes with Josh,**
Box 1000, Dallas, TX 75221

ADDITIONAL JOSH McDOWELL RESOURCES FROM WORD PUBLISHING

BOOKS

Don't Check Your Brains at the Door
How to Help Your Child Say "No" to Sexual Pressure
How to Be a Hero to Your Kids
Love, Dad
Under Seige
Unlocking the Secrets of Being Loved, Accepted, and Secure

AUDIO

How to Help Your Child Say "No" to Sexual Pressure
How to Be a Hero to Your Kids
"No!"—The Positive Answer (Love Waiting Music)
The Secret of Loving
The Teenage Q&A Book on Tape
Why Wait: What You Need to Know about the Teen
    Sexuality Crisis
Why Waiting Is Worth the Wait

VIDEOS AND VIDEO CURRICULUM

A Clean Heart for a New Start
Don't Check Your Brains at the Door
Evidence for Faith
God Is No Cosmic Kill-Joy
How to Handle the Pressure Lines
How to Help Your Child Say "No" to Sexual Pressure
Let's Talk about Love and Sex
The Myths of Sex Education
"No!"—The Positive Answer
See You at the Party
The Teenage Q&A Video Series
Where Youth Are Today
Who Do You Listen To?
Why Waiting Is Worth the Wait

GOING TO COLLEGE?
Don't Go It Alone

Some new Christian friends are already waiting to meet you!!

To connect with Christians and campus ministers at your college, contact Student LINC toll free at 1-800-678-LINC (5462).

Student LINC provides a centralized database where Campus Crusade for Christ, InterVarsity Christian Fellowship, and the Navigators have pooled their information about the locations of their ministries on campuses across the United Staes.

Student LINC can give you the name and phone number of the leader for each group on campus.

Also, if no strong Christian group is active on your campus, Student LINC can help you start one. For more information, just give them a call at 1-800-678-LINC (5462).

Don't leave home before calling!

OPERATION POWERLINK

PowerLink is a national evangelistic outreach campaign for youth groups across the nation. Youth groups will be participating in a video series outreach training course in preparation for inviting their non-Christian friends to their own locally sponsored "See You At the Party" event on March 6, 1993. The vision is that some fifty thousand youth groups across the nation will simultaneously conduct their own "See You At the Party" outreach by viewing a live-by-satellite broadcast featuring contemporary Christian music and a message by Josh McDowell.

In addition to *Thirteen Things You Gotta Know*, you will also want to look for the **PowerLink Video Series**, a package of two videos (containing six sessions) featuring contemporary Christian music and testimonies by Josh McDowell and others. The video pack includes a copy of *Under Seige*, a leader's guide, this devotional book, and *The PowerLink Youth Bible*.

The PowerLink Youth Bible is translated for today's teen and is based on the acclaimed, easy-to-read New Century Version. Added sidelights and real-life stories make this a powerful Bible that speaks to youth.

Available at your Christian bookstore

ABOUT THE AUTHORS

Josh McDowell is an internationally known speaker, author, and traveling representative for Campus Crusade for Christ. A graduate of Wheaton College and Talbot Theological Seminary, he has written more than thirty-five books and appeared in numerous films, videos, and television series. He and his wife Dottie, live in Julian, California, with their four children.

Bob Hostetler is a writer, editor, and frequent speaker at writers' conferences and churches. He co-authored with Josh McDowell *Don't Check Your Brains at the Door* and has published hundreds of articles, sermons, stories and cartoons. Bob edited the national youth publications for The Salvation Army for four years and has served as a pastor in churches in Ohio. He and his wife Robin, have ministered together as house parents to troubled teenagers and now live in Southwestern Ohio with their daughter, Aubrey, and son, Aaron.